while YOU wait

FINDING PURPOSE IN THE "NOT YETS"

JERRY MEEK

FOREWORD BY KYLE BROWNLEE

HIGH BRIDGE BOOKS

HOUSTON

While You Wait
by Jerry Meek

Printed in the United States of America
ISBN: 978-1-954943-54-4

Team DSC®, Personal Resorts®, The DSC Standard®, Building the Best Better®, and Builder for Life® are registered service marks of Desert Star Construction, Inc. The author has used these service marks within this book with permission from Desert Star Construction, Inc.

Scripture quotations marked NIV are taken from THE HOLY BIBLE, NEW INTERNATIONAL VERSION®, NIV® Copyright © 1973, 1978, 1984, 2011 by Biblica, Inc.® Used by permission. All rights reserved worldwide.

Scripture quotations marked MSG are taken from THE MESSAGE, copyright © 1993, 2002, 2018 by Eugene H. Peterson. Used by permission of NavPress. All rights reserved. Represented by Tyndale House Publishers, Inc.

Scripture quotations marked NASB are taken from New American Standard Bible®, Copyright © 1960, 1971, 1977, 1995, 2020 by The Lockman Foundation. All rights reserved.

Scripture quotations marked NLT are taken from the Holy Bible, New Living Translation, copyright © 1996, 2004, 2015 by Tyndale House Foundation. Used by permission of Tyndale House Publishers, Inc., Carol Stream, Illinois 60188. All rights reserved.

Scripture quotations marked KJV are taken from The Authorized (King James) Version of the Bible ('the KJV'). The rights which are vested in the Crown in the United Kingdom is reproduced here by permission of the Crown's patentee, Cambridge University Press.

Scripture quotations marked NKJV are taken from the New King James Version®. Copyright © 1982 by Thomas Nelson. Used by permission. All rights reserved.

Scripture quotations marked NCV are taken from the New Century Version®. Copyright © 2005 by Thomas Nelson. Used by permission. All rights reserved.

Scripture quotations marked TLB are taken from The Living Bible copyright © 1971 by Tyndale House Foundation. Used by permission of Tyndale House Publishers Inc., Carol Stream, Illinois 60188. All rights reserved. The Living Bible, TLB, and the The Living Bible logo are registered trademarks of Tyndale House Publishers.

High Bridge Books titles may be purchased in bulk for educational, business, fundraising, or sales promotional use. For information, please contact High Bridge Books via www.HighBridge-Books.com/contact.

Published in Houston, Texas by High Bridge Books.

To my parents, Ida J. and Gerald E. Meek, who waited through adversity and during some of life's most significant challenges and finished victorious as examples of lives changed through Christ.

Also by Jerry Meek

Leadership on the Level

Be Great... Before It's Too Late

Teambuilder Toolbox: 13 Tools to Build the Power of Your Team

The LORD answered me: "Write down the vision; write it clearly on clay tablets so whoever reads it can run to tell others. It is not yet time for the message to come true, but that time is coming soon; the message will come true. It may seem like a long time, but be patient and wait for it, because it will surely come; it will not be delayed."

—Habakkuk 2:2-3 NCV

Contents

Foreword

I've heard it said that in life, it's not what you know but *who* you know that leads to success. I've been fortunate enough to have some incredible Christian, and non-Christian, leaders come into my life and help me get to where I am today. They have helped me overcome things I wasn't sure I could overcome and encouraged me to keep going when I felt like giving up and to be better tomorrow than I am today.

I've discovered that the people who have the greatest impact on our lives aren't the people we believe in but the people who believe in us. That's one of the many things I love about Jerry Meek—he truly loves and believes in people. In fact, from the moment I met Jerry at a gathering of pastors and business leaders in Vail, Colorado, he has been cheering me on and challenging me not to settle but to be all that God has created me to be.

We've all found ourselves between where we are and where we want to be. That's why this book is so important—the decisions we make today will determine what kind of lives we live tomorrow. That's what's so special about the book you're holding: It's a testament to the size of Jerry's heart that he wishes to see people overcome adversity and reach their full potential.

In Ephesians 5:16, the Apostle Paul told us to make the most of every opportunity. Throughout this book, Jerry helps us recognize that our obstacles are opportunities: opportunities for a more significant victory, greater freedom, a greater purpose, and ultimately a more extraordinary relationship with God. I love how Jerry shares the experiences that helped him over the years, not focusing on the size of our struggles but on the size of our God.

While pastoring for almost twenty years, I've seen so many people shrink back in the struggle and grow weary in the waiting. That's why I'm so thankful for this book. God wants to impart something on the inside of you that would cause you to rise up and run through any obstacle that's in front of you. I encourage you to not just read this book but let it inspire you to go to a place you've never been before. God is about to do something extraordinary in your life.

—**Kyle Brownlee**
Pastor, Xperience Church
Defiance, Ohio

Introduction

One of life's certainties is that we are either waiting or will spend our time waiting for something. Whether it's for an undelivered package, in a long line at the grocery store, or for the traffic light to turn green, we're undoubtedly rushing somewhere. I've done my fair share of waiting during my 44 years in the construction business for things outside my direct control. We wait for plans to be complete so we can build, wait for client decisions, and wait for unique items coming from overseas, such as windows, tile, stone, and concrete. If I'm honest, I have also found myself losing patience with those around me during the waiting. I'm not the type to sit around and do nothing. I'm results-oriented, constantly thinking about and wanting to move on to what's next.

Being the CEO of our construction company affords me a particular ability to keep things moving in my world. Still, I've also had to wrestle with waiting seasons beyond my control and far outside my comfort zone. Recently, my wife Carol suffered a rare but severe heart attack, and we spent much of the following year anxiously waiting on a prognosis and finding out her next steps. During this season, I thought a lot about waiting—why we wait, what we wait on, what we do during the waiting, etc. Specifically, I had been focusing on distinguishing between waiting on something urgent and something significant.

As Dwight D. Eisenhower put it, "What is important is seldom urgent, and what is urgent is seldom important" (Quote Investigator). During a water leak, the water must be immediately shut off at the source to stop the flow and minimize incurred damage.

...the important things rarely come quickly.

Of course, we all have urgent day-to-day matters to attend to, but they rarely have a high impact on our life. What's important are the things that align with the vision we have for our life and add value to it—and the important things rarely come quickly.

Many of us, myself included, would say that we clearly understand the distinction. But I often get far too wrapped up and emotionally invested in the *urgent*, taking my time and energy away from the *important*. While reading *Bearing God's Name* by Carmine Joy Imes—who earned a Ph.D. in biblical theology and is an associate professor of Old Testament at Prairie College in Alberta, Canada—I learned a new word: **liminal**. When I researched the word, I realized we are in a liminal state while waiting. We are waiting on what's next. In short, the liminal space is where we leave something behind, yet we are not entirely in our next season.

God spoke to me amid all this waiting and thinking about urgency versus importance and reminded me that, whether I like it or not, waiting is an absolute certainty. No matter what stage of life, we are all waiting in some liminal or transitional state. Whether that's a recent college graduate waiting on their first job or an engaged couple waiting to be married. Perhaps it's nine months waiting for a pregnant mother to finally hold her child or someone waiting on a health diagnosis, as I previously mentioned.

But what do we do in the waiting? I believe what matters to God is not that we wait but *how* we wait. Do we spend our time fearful and anxious, pursuing everything we think is urgent and nothing truly important? Do we press into God, allow him to grow our character, and learn from whatever season of waiting we find ourselves in?

After spending many years in the construction business, I've started to see how the building process relates to life: the importance of a strong foundation, good infrastructure to allow for future expansion, and the beauty of interior finishes. Lately, I've focused on the imagery of the door, specifically the threshold. (Yes, that little strip of wood, metal, or stone that forms the bottom of a doorway). A door is a solid barrier between two environments. It remains closed to protect and hold elements from each side until the appointed time comes to allow passage or participation between the two sides. There is a purpose in what is happening on each side of the door, but timing and preparation are important to determine when the door opens and closes, how long it takes to pass through, and when it closes.

Throughout the Bible, we read about standing at the threshold of a door and knocking. In the book of Matthew, Jesus said:

> Ask and it will be given to you; seek and you will find; knock and the door will be opened to you. For everyone who asks receives; the one who seeks finds; and to the one who knocks, the door will be opened. (7:7-8 NIV)

We see countless times when God literally and figuratively opened doors for His children. In Acts, Paul and Silas were imprisoned, praying and singing hymns to God. All the prison doors flew open at once, and everyone's chains came loose (Acts 16:25-26).

We also see Jesus refer to Himself as the door. In John, Jesus said, "I am the door: by me if any man enter in, he shall be saved, and shall go in and out, and find pasture" (John 10:9 KJV).

The book of Revelation tells us that Jesus stands at the door of our hearts and knocks. Throughout the Bible, we see powerful imagery of doors waiting to be answered and opened. It reminds me that we are all also in a season of waiting at the threshold of what's next.

But God doesn't want us to get ahead of Him. He opens doors that only He can open and no one can shut, and He shuts doors that no one can open (Rev. 3:7 and Isa. 22:22). His timing is perfect. Regardless of our life stage, how we wait is determined by our perspective of our experiences, lessons learned from previous seasons of waiting, and our trust in God's Word. Do we want what we want when we want it? Or do we press into God, trusting He's doing good work within us, preparing us for all He has in store on the other side of whatever door we are waiting at?

Though my natural inclination is not one of patience, I have spent my recent seasons of waiting diving into God's Word and studying how some prominent figures in biblical history responded during their season(s) of waiting. What were they waiting on? How did they wait? What did God teach them? What can we learn from them?

In *While You Wait*, I attempt to share what I've learned along my journey, combining stories from my own life with the lessons learned from spending time in God's Word. To encourage your participation, I have also included a takeaway section to list lessons learned from the chapter and a reflection section with questions to help readers dig deeper into their waiting seasons. I hope you'll join me as we learn from and are encouraged by those in the Bible. Like us, they have experienced their seasons of waiting at the threshold.

1

At the Threshold

Many aspects of construction also relate specifically to how we build our lives: step by step, with an intentional design, specific components for desired functionality, and a timeline to get it done so we can occupy it and maximize what happens within it for the best possible results. As mentioned before, I learned a new word after reading *Bearing God's Name* by Carmine Joy Imes: liminal—meaning intermediate or transitional. "Limen" is even a synonym for threshold.

This new word and its relation to building structures immediately stuck out. I felt like God kept tugging at me, reminding me that we are in a liminal transition state when we are waiting at the threshold of something new. In architecture, liminality can refer to transitional or transformational spaces. Transitions can be hallways or an elevator that takes you up to the desired floor, down to the basement, or to the parking garage.

I find it interesting that "limen" can be used interchangeably with "threshold," that strip of wood, metal, stone, or other material that forms the bottom of a doorway.

This was the liminal God put on my heart and one of the inspirations for writing this book about waiting!

Before we get too deep, let's take a quick look at the threshold. In medieval times, it was a board anchored to the floors to prevent straw, dust, and rainwater from being blown inside by the wind. In England, it was common to spread "thresh" (probably reeds or rushes) on the home's floor to prevent slipping, necessitating a piece of wood at the bottom of the doorway to hold the thresh inside. Its most literal definition has three simple uses for a threshold. It keeps things out, it keeps things in, and is a barrier that must be crossed over to step into or out of a space.

...any time we are waiting at the threshold of something new, we are also in a liminal transition state.

My wife Carol and I live in Arizona, where the desert has its own unique environment. Some days we are keeping out summer heat in excess of 120 degrees, yet we had snow in a recent winter! I just want to keep out the snakes and scorpions.

On the other hand, when we first moved to Arizona in the late 1960s, there was no air conditioning. We used an evaporative cooler, which was great until the monsoon season. Then it became ineffective due to high humidity. For our current desert-dwelling, we want to keep in the air-conditioned climate. We also want to keep in the clean air, which keeps out the dust and fends off viruses.

Perhaps the essential aspect of a threshold is crossing over it. No matter the season we are in or at what door of life we find ourselves standing, we can consider the threshold as a boundary or the end of a runway, a place to cross over—in other words, the place where we enter a new beginning. As you step over the threshold, you're transitioning from one space to another, and the spiritual implications and imagery aren't lost on me.

I've had many liminal periods in my life: when I was engaged to be married, and after seven years of marriage, Carol was pregnant with our first son, Jeremy. In both instances, we were in transition, unmarried and not parents yet. We knew that both times would come one day, but for the time being, we were waiting in the space between for what came next.

Significant health issues affected me during my thirties, with severe leg pain leaving me unable to walk for eighteen months. The doctors performed countless tests, but they revealed no answers. The final autopsy was the only other test they could think of. I said no thanks; I will wait. Waiting to be better and mobile again was a difficult period for me. I just wanted to go on with my everyday life, stop talking or thinking about it, and so I chose day by day to do that. At the end of a week, I realized the pain seemed to be subsiding. I thanked God and decided I didn't need to know how or what transpired but was just thankful and would keep moving forward.

Most recently, my seemingly healthy wife suffered two heart attacks (diagnosed as SCAD—spontaneous coronary artery dissection) just two days after our fortieth wedding anniversary.

We renewed our vows three days ahead of Carol's first heart attack. She asked whether I would have renewed them if I knew what was coming. My answer was absolutely yes.

If we had waited, it might not have taken place. As I write this, we are still in a liminal state of waiting for her recovery and total healing from three artery dissections, which are 100 percent blocked. No travel, no altitude, and we wait one year to see how well she recuperates. In the liminal space of waiting patiently and hopefully, what is God doing within us, how is our character being shaped and further refined, and what future life pathway is He redefining or redirecting?

Being in a liminal space while waiting for answers on my wife's health has influenced the speeches I've been blessed to give at private and public universities and colleges. Depending on the venue, I will either share my faith or talk about leadership principles and my experiences with success in the construction business. Sometimes I get to share both.

Regardless of the venue, when I look out at the students, I see that they are all in a liminal state. Students are beginning their journey through college or stepping over the threshold and into the professional world on the other side. As they graduate, they have to choose which direction to take next. I hope to help them (and readers) understand that this is an ongoing journey. Throughout life, we will have many threshold moments, and the quicker we learn to embrace these times of transition and waiting, the better prepared we will be for what lies on the other side of these doors of opportunity.

The threshold is critical, regardless of the material. A threshold must be tall enough to function but low enough not to be a tripping hazard. One of its primary functions is keeping out the bad and keeping in the good. I can't help but think about how this relates to our daily lives. What do we need to keep out of our lives to stay healthy and prosperous? Social media, television, or toxic relationships? (Maybe all three and more!)

I can't stress enough the importance of staying out of the comparison trap (2 Cor. 10:12) and learning to lay down past failures and disappointments so that you're free to embrace what's next.

While it may be uncomfortable, what we do in the waiting prepares us to cross over the threshold and step into all that God has in store for our next season. How we wait matters. (Hint: the answer isn't quitting!)

What do we desperately need to keep in our lives? I am passionate about spending time in God's Word and developing relationships with people who will support me and challenge me to be the best version of myself. At Desert Star Construction (DSC), it's been said we have a high threshold and barrier to entry. We don't let just anyone work on our projects; we seek out those who are endeavoring to be the best at what they do. I have a high threshold for pain. (My appendix was removed after thinking it was just a stomachache!) When the pain of life comes, we can choose to be resilient, embrace the pain, and start recovery. In pressing through difficulties, we become resourceful to find innovative solutions, stronger than we thought possible, and prepared for what comes next. In overcoming, we develop character and faith with the reality that difficult things will come, but we can face them and emerge stronger.

We all experience different thresholds in our lives, and heroes of the faith and prominent people throughout the Bible were not immune to waiting either. In Psalm 40:1-2, King David spoke about his struggles with waiting and the necessity of relying on God during those times:

> I waited patiently for the Lord;
>   he turned to me and heard my cry.
> He lifted me out of the slimy pit,
>   out of the mud and mire;
> he set my feet on a rock
>   and gave me a firm place to stand. (NIV)

God can and will listen to us if we wait patiently, and He will lift us to a solid, firm place where we can stand. His timing may not be as immediate as you would want if you are like me (or King David). You may feel you are constantly waiting, standing at the door bound by mud and slime, stuck in a pit. This created an image of being stuck in quicksand, unable to make progress, and in danger of sinking. (The harder I struggle in my power, the quicker I sink and the more stuck I become!) David waited patiently, even while in the pit, until he heard from God.

The choices we make in the waiting will go a long way in determining when and to what degree of success we can take our next step.

King Solomon, David's son, considered to be one of the wisest people in history, said, "There's an opportune time to do things, a right time for everything on the earth." (Eccl. 3:1 MSG) Pastor Jentezen Franklin, said, "Of all the things that King Solomon wrote about, he never mentioned a *time to quit.*"

The point? These wise men of God remind us that our waiting period is just a single moment in time. While it may be uncomfortable, what we do in the waiting prepares us to cross over the threshold and step into all God has in store for our next season. *(Hint: the answer isn't quitting!) How we wait matters.*

I wasn't sure that God guided my steps during my early years in business. Everything was so difficult; I often wondered where I missed the fork in the road. One thing I learned was that God was creating a tapestry I could not see. Every experience, project, and person I worked with was part of my journey. The foundation was being laid that nobody could see yet.

God created each of us and designed us for a unique purpose. Looking back, I realize if God had shown me what was ahead, I would not have been ready for it. In most cases, I wasn't prepared emotionally, spiritually, or financially to embrace the future. I had to spend time in the waiting as He prepared me for all that was to come. I learned how to process disappointment and move on without being angry or bitter. Afterward, I realized not getting certain projects was God's protection from situations not in our best interest. I learned how to communicate to create successful outcomes embraced by the team—in other instances, waiting allowed not good projects but the best projects to come.

Understanding that we are all waiting for something is only half the equation. The choices we make in the waiting will go a long way in determining when and to what degree of success we can take our next step.

How will you spend your time in the waiting?

Takeaways

1. Throughout life, we will have many threshold moments. It's important to embrace these moments of waiting and do your best to prepare for what's next.

2. While you wait, think about what you need to let go of and what to incorporate more of in this season of life.

Reflections

1. What season of transition and waiting are you currently in? Take a few minutes and define yours—is it relational, emotional, professional, or spiritual?

_____

_____

_____

_____

_____

_____

2. How can you learn to embrace your time at the threshold practically?

_____

_____

_____

_____

_____

_____

3. Make a list of things you need to keep out of your life so you can take your next step. Make another list of what you need more of in your life.

_____

_____

_____

_____

_____

_____

_____

2

You Are a Masterpiece

In 2006, real estate developer and art collector Steve Wynn agreed to sell his original Picasso painting, *Le Rêve*, for $135 million. He threw a "goodbye party" for his painting at his Wynn Resort in Las Vegas. Unfortunately, as he turned to look at his masterpiece during the party, he inadvertently put his elbow through it, tearing a hole in the painting the size of a silver dollar. As you can probably guess, the sale was canceled. Steve suffers from macular degeneration.

But the story doesn't end there. Steve paid $90,000 to have his painting restored, and in 2013, the buyer who had backed out from the previous sale in 2006 bought the painting for $155 million. It turns out that, just seven years later, the damaged version of *Le Rêve* was worth $20 million more than the original. Remodel an old house, and the value consistently increases. Very few masterpieces are pristine. If inspected, many of the old master's paintings would reveal the original had been repaired. It is no different than a painting, except the painting appreciates more.

Over the years, we've built homes for many clients who collect art and display it on their walls. On more than one occasion, I've been asked to move a Monet or a Rembrandt. To say I was intimidated to handle those priceless pieces is a massive understatement. It seemed unbelievable to me that a damaged Picasso sold for more than its undamaged previous self, but through my work in construction, I later learned a bit about the value of paintings.

After moving a few valuable and historically significant paintings, I asked my clients why they chose a particular piece and what made it valuable. Their responses intrigued me. They chose works based on their significance but also understood the importance of properly maintaining them to ensure they grew in value. I was also frequently told that they were suitable long-term investments.

While many factors influence the value of a masterpiece, the most compelling answer I received was the value of authenticity versus a reproduction or copy.

> *While many factors influence the value of a masterpiece, the most compelling answer I received was the value of authenticity versus a reproduction or copy.*

The idea of authenticity influencing the value of a work reminds me of how God references us as His creations. In Ephesians 2:10, Paul said, "For we are God's handiwork, created in Christ Jesus to do good works, which God prepared in advance for us to do" (NIV). British scholar F.F. Bruce even referred to humanity as God's "work of art, His masterpiece." Human beings as art? As God's masterpieces? (The New Living Translation even translates it this way in

Ephesians 2:10!) Could there be a more beautiful, eye-opening description than that?

> *"Your worth as a person has to do with your value. Your value is not based on what you do, but who made you."*
>
> *– Richard E. Simmons III*

So if we are masterpieces, created uniquely by God, what does that say about us?

In his book, *The True Measure of a Man*, Richard E. Simmons III wrote, "Your worth as a person has to do with your value. Your value is not based on what you do, but who made you." We are all valuable because God makes us. Unless you are painting by numbers, the painter and not the canvas create the painting.

> *We are all valuable because God makes us.*

But God doesn't just create us to put us on display. He also has a great plan that's unique for each of us.

Tony Evans said it this way:

Although you're not saved by good works, you are saved for good works. We are His workmanship, Paul says, created in Christ Jesus for good works. When it comes to your salvation, God is crafting your life into a piece of art. He is working on you and doing something with you. You are being re-created to do good works. A good work is a divinely prescribed action that benefits others in such a way that God is glorified. (See Matthew 5:16)

But what does any of this have to do with waiting? It is important to understand and know your value. You are unique, and God set you apart for such a time as this. No one else alive or in history has the same gifts, talents, and experiences as you do. If you don't truly understand your value and see yourself as God sees you, you will end up stuck in a void and wander without direction or purpose. Or you will jump at the first opportunity you see instead of waiting for the door that God opens just for you.

For example, I didn't fully understand my uniqueness until much later in life. My family moved a lot when I was young, and I had attended ten different schools by the time I finished high school. While we lived in California, my dad worked with my uncle, a building designer. I was fascinated by the building world and was excited to become an architect.

No one else alive or in history has the same gifts, talents, and experiences as you do.

I enrolled in a drafting class in high school and felt I was doing an above-average job until my teacher suggested that, with handwriting like mine, I should transfer to shop class. Penmanship is essential, and my letters and numbers needed improvement to be legible. I wasn't thrilled with my teacher's response. I later discovered my calling when I started a carpentry business with my father, which soon grew into DSC, one of the market's leading custom luxury home building businesses. As a general contractor, it has been an honor, a privilege, and an enormous responsibility to complete the projects we have for our clients over the last forty-four years. I found who God made me to be, and I couldn't be happier than when I'm walking in my calling.

> ## If you don't truly understand your value and see yourself as God sees you, you will end up waiting in vain forever.

Many people are dissatisfied simply because they haven't gotten around to God's work. In fact, at the 2020 GrowLeader Conference, which "resources high-capacity leaders to reach their full potential so churches and businesses can reach more people," Pastor Chris Hodges shared a concerning statistic: 87% of people will never know their purpose. Don't be one of the 87% who is unfulfilled! But when you understand the grace with which God saved you, gratitude will drive your response to Him and His plans.

Reach your highest value by being your authentic and best self. You are not worth nearly as much if you are a copy of someone else. Invest your life into something significant and rare to maintain and grow your value. But remember that the increased value comes over time, and you'll need to spiritually, physically, and emotionally invest in yourself along the way.

> *When you understand the grace with which God saved you, gratitude will drive your response to Him and His plans.*

God cares about the big things and the little things in our lives. His promises indicate that He has a plan and will carry it out (Jer. 29:11). In our times of unknowing, adversity, loneliness, and waiting, God wants us to be more concerned about His plan for our good. No matter what you have experienced in your life or what you are waiting on, God is waiting for you with open and loving arms to welcome you.

> *Reach your highest value by being your authentic and best self.*

You and I are God's works of art—we are His masterpieces!

I encourage you to look in the mirror (seriously, take a look in your mirror) and remind yourself that you are God's masterpiece, created in His image and that He has a unique plan for your life. "For we are God's masterpiece. He has created us anew in Christ Jesus, so we can do the good things he planned for us long ago" (Eph. 2:10 NLT). Take this moment and ask God to put you in a place, maybe with a new job or environment, where you are fulfilled and energized. You may be in the wrong class like I was, but you can get to the right one.

Takeaways

1. Know your value by reflecting on who God has created you to be.

2. Trust that God has great plans for you—He will see you fully through them.

3. Ask God to put you in a place where you are fulfilled and energized in all that you do.

Reflections

1. What does the story about *Le Rêve's* sale make you think about the value of authenticity?

_____

_____

_____

_____

_____

_____

2. Do you see yourself as uniquely gifted and talented? Take a moment to list your strengths and abilities. How can you use your gifts in your time of waiting?

_____

_____

_____

_____

_____

_____

3. Are you walking and growing in your God-given calling? If not, what next step can you take toward growing closer to your destiny?

_____

_____

_____

_____

_____

_____

3

Cattle and Bison

A few years ago, my wife, Carol, and I were visiting Jackson Hole, Wyoming, with our construction peer group. After several days of meetings, we decided to drive through the breathtaking countryside and take in the sights. As we drove, I noticed bison along the roads and was quickly fascinated by these creatures. Approaching the next herd, I pulled over to take a closer look. I did everything I could to scare them into motion but to no avail. After taking a few pictures, I realized these giant creatures now blocking the road weren't going anywhere anytime soon.

As Carol laughed at my antics (yelling and jumping) and ultimate failure in moving the bison, storm clouds moved in, and the rain began to pour. What happened next was fascinating and stayed with me long after that day. A group of cows came into sight, and it became apparent they were running away from the coming storm. The bison, on the other hand, remained stationary.

As the rain came down harder and we retreated to the safety of our car, the cows ran frantically from the rain, thunder, and lightning, seemingly unaware of the bison. But the bison remained rooted to their spots. I did not anticipate that the bison would do the exact opposite of the cows. Of all things, the bison turned and began moving toward the storm.

It was an "ah-ha" God moment for me. I quickly realized that as the cows were running from the storm, they would end up struggling to escape it and get caught in it until it passed. The bison, heading into the storm, would be in it for a much shorter time.

I can't help but think of the story of Jonah and how he fled from the calling God placed on his life. But also, due to his own choices, how he likely spent much longer amid his storm than needed.

> *Fortunately, God can and will use the storms and trials to grow us, build our character, and redirect us to where He wants us.*

During Jonah's lifetime, Nineveh was a city completely at odds with God's ways. In response to their wandering, God called Jonah, an Old Testament prophet, to travel to Nineveh and encourage their repentance while warning of their coming destruction. Jonah had other ideas. He didn't think Nineveh was worth saving. Instead of sharing the Word of God with their neighbors, Jonah and the Israelites expected God to destroy those who didn't know Him. They had their expectations of how God would act and were waiting for Him to meet those expectations.

Because of these beliefs about Nineveh, he avoided his assigned mission. Instead of heeding God's call, Jonah avoided his assigned mission at all costs. He ran to the coast and caught a ride on a ship going in the opposite direction of where God had called him. The ship was battered by storms until the other passengers, thinking it was Jonah's fault, threw him overboard (Jonah 2:10). Jonah asked the sailors to throw him overboard because he knew the storm was for him. Then Jonah was swallowed by a giant fish and spent three days and nights in the belly of the beast before it spat him up on the shore within a three-day walk to Nineveh, the country he was fleeing (Jonah 3:1-3)!

> *The calling God places on our lives rarely makes us comfortable. It will require us to stretch and to have faith in Him.*

One way or another, Jonah was going to Nineveh, but I wonder how much longer and more difficult his journey was due to his attitude toward God's call on his life. Like the cows I noticed, Jonah spent his time running from the inevitable and spent considerable time in precarious positions amid wild storms. Jonah caused his season of waiting through disobedience. Jonah is an example of what to avoid, and his disobedience delayed God's ultimate plan.

> *We'll never know how many people we can impact for eternity if we're constantly running from the storms that are so important in shaping us!*

I'm not claiming that God causes all our trials or the heartaches and circumstances we face. We have an enemy who is out to kill, steal, and destroy (John 10:10), but we can also often cause our own storms when we flee from the direction God is calling us. Fortunately, God can and will use the storms and trials to grow us, build our character, and redirect us to where He wants us:

> ...so that the proof of your faith, being more precious than gold which is perishable, even though tested by fire, may be found to result in praise and glory and honor at the revelation of Jesus Christ; (1 Pet. 1:7 NASB)

The calling God places on our lives rarely makes us comfortable. It will require us to stretch and to have faith in Him. Faith needs to grow and stretch like our muscles to get stronger. We are on a journey in our relationship with Christ to grow and mature to become like Him. Stretching our faith is like Jonah's experience. He had no desire to step out of his comfort zone and travel to Nineveh to preach the gospel to unbelievers. But God had more excellent plans than Jonah's comfort. Through Jonah, and even at times despite him, God ultimately redeemed 120,000 people in Nineveh. In the end, Jonah was shaped by his storms, and God pricked his heart for the lost:

> But I, with shouts of grateful praise, will sacrifice to you. What I have vowed I will make good. I will say, 'Salvation comes from the LORD.' (Jonah 2:9 NIV)

God's timing is always perfect. Have you ever stopped and reflected on your life's seasons of waiting? Rather than listening to God, did you ever go a different direction and delay what God wanted to accomplish through and for you?

As with Jonah, God has a unique plan that will likely ask us to step into unfamiliar or uncomfortable territory. Let's take a page out of the bison's playbook and press forward toward God's calling, allowing whatever storms we face to refine us and grow our faith and dependence on Him.

As we do, we can find peace and joy in knowing that God's timing is perfect and His purpose for our life is far greater than we can imagine. Remember—we will never know how many people we can impact for eternity if we're constantly running from the storms that are so important in shaping us!

> The meaning of waiting in both the Old and New Testaments is "standing under," actively enduring. It is not standing with folded arms doing nothing. It is not saying, "In God's good time, it will come to pass." By that, we often mean, "In my abominably lazy time, I let God work." Waiting means standing under, in active strength, enduring till the answer comes. (Oswald Chambers)

Takeaways

1. The length of your waiting period is unknown, but what can be certain is the attitude you choose while you wait.

2. God uses our waiting to develop our character and prepare us for what is ahead—He has a purpose in every season of our lives.

3. God's timing is always perfect. Remind yourself of this truth as you reflect on prior seasons of waiting in your life.

4. Be the bison—boldly face the storms with trust and perseverance.

Reflections

1. Has God placed a calling on your life that you've yet to pursue? Take a moment to prayerfully ask God what steps He wants you to take next.

_____

_____

_____

_____

_____

2. How has God previously grown your character during times of trial? What did He teach you that you can apply now?

_____

_____

_____

_____

_____

_____

_____

3. Are you in the middle of a storm? Instead of running from it and seeking comfort, ask God what He wants you to learn and for the strength to walk confidently through it.

_____

_____

_____

_____

_____

_____

4

Right vs. Right Now

Recently, I was scheduled to attend a wedding across the country. I was friends with the bride's family and knew the couple getting married. I had committed to attend what was a very important day for our friends, but two days before we were scheduled to fly across the country, my dad's health took a turn for the worse.

I began to justify why attending the wedding was important. I'd committed, and keeping my word has always been my priority. Nobody would judge me if something happened while I was away and I missed my father's passing.

My next thought was about who I could call for advice. As I drove home from work for the day, God reminded me that I didn't need to call a single person for advice. I needed to talk to Him. As I drove along the highway, God brought Proverbs 3:5-6 to mind:

> Trust GOD from the bottom of your heart;
> don't try to figure out everything on your own.
> Listen for GOD's voice in everything you do,
> everywhere you go; he's the one who will keep
> you on track. (MSG)

Earlier in the month, I'd read the Tony Evans Bible commentary on this verse that said you could see a person's faith by observing where they turn first for advice. God desires us to seek Him first in everything, and as I brought this decision to Him, He immediately gave me clarity. He wanted me to be with my dad and be there for my family. I was thankful that my friend and her family understood my absence.

Little did I know that my dad was close to death, and these final days with him would be irreplaceable. I am so grateful that God helped me understand the difference and choose what was important over what seemed urgent to me at the time.

I can't help but think I was struggling with a little bit of Martha's mindset from when she and her sister Mary waited on a visiting Jesus (See Luke 10). While they were both fully devoted followers of Jesus, their decisions and attitudes during times of waiting couldn't have been more different. Like anyone, they had unique personalities and were blessed with different strengths, and how each responded to the presence of Jesus can teach us a great deal about waiting.

Part of the learning process is embracing patience. We can grow weary while we wait, but we should always endure through the periods of "Not Yet." Wait for God's best for you.

Martha had the gift of hospitality. When she saw Jesus approaching, she acted and invited him into her home. She immediately went to work to ensure that the food and setting were perfect for Jesus and His disciples. No doubt this took much work, skill, and a lot of focus. Martha focused on Jesus' comfort, and it must have been a frenzy of energy for her. Mary, known as a worshiper, desired to sit and learn at the feet of Jesus. After all, the dinner was for Jesus.

Not every good thing is a God thing.

While Mary and Martha were loving sisters, they were still human. Martha was not only angry with Mary; it seems that she was also frustrated with Jesus for not reprimanding her sister. Martha worked so hard to accommodate the visitors and ensure their comfort, yet Mary wasn't helping; she was just sitting there. How could Jesus not see and appreciate the difference in Martha's sense of responsibility and Mary's desire to wait in His presence? Jesus' response was telling:

> The Master said, "Martha, dear Martha, you're fussing far too much and getting yourself worked up over nothing. One thing only is essential, and Mary has chosen it—it's the main course, and won't be taken from her."
> (Luke 10:41-42 MSG)

Mary and Martha possessed different gifts, each important in their own way. But Martha let the urgency of her responsibilities in the kitchen take priority over what was truly important. Jesus knew his time on earth was limited, but Martha didn't. She spent her energy focusing on the short-term in front of her, on what she decided was important, and missed the opportunity to sit and learn at the feet of Jesus, whose Word will never fail or be taken away (1 Pet. 1:25).

Martha missed the main thing! She believed without a doubt that waiting on and serving her guests was the most crucial task. She was wrong. Martha confused activity with advancement and motion with actual movement. I highly doubt Martha would have been so concerned with food and table settings had she known that Jesus' days were numbered. Her priorities would have shifted to fellowship with Jesus, the true source of fulfillment. But she didn't slow down enough to find out if all her serving was what Jesus wanted her to be doing. Mary knew the importance of sitting at Jesus' feet was the priority and learning everything that she could.

> *Are we first attending to what we see as urgent, or are we taking a step back to lean into what God says is truly important?*

This story reminds me of the importance of seeking God's voice as we wait. It also reminds me that not every good thing is a God thing. This is truly the only way to discern between what we may see as important but is merely urgent in the grand scheme of things and the truth of God's calling and His next steps for us.

These sisters also make me think about many of the true successes our team at DSC has seen. Much, if not all, of our success is due to defining and working on our priorities to lead the trade contractors and meet or exceed client expectations of quality, budget, and schedule. If we're not careful, we can get so caught up in being active and completing tasks that we don't realize that we're not contributing to the vision of what's important.

Nothing was wrong with Martha serving Jesus. In fact, it was a good thing. In and of itself, completing our tasks is a good thing, too. But it's the difference between doing what's right now versus doing what's right in the long run.

If we're doing the right thing, the smaller next steps become simple and clear. We also have the added peace that comes with knowing that our focus is in the right place.

Practically, for each construction project, our team sits down and decides what's important, and then we decide what we can do right now to gain momentum toward that goal. The smaller next steps become straightforward if we're doing the right thing. We also have the added peace of knowing that our focus is in the right place.

Growing up, many of us learned nuggets of wisdom from parents or friends that we still remember and apply. One that comes to mind is "desperation knows no choice." When we are desperate, we can jump at the first thing that comes our way. This applies to friendships, what job to pursue, and defining decision points in life, who to marry. I advise you to never compromise your future to satisfy your present—never!"

While we wait, we will have many opportunities for activity. Building your life is like creating a project. One example is the foundation. Having a well-engineered foundation to handle the final structure is critical. Have you considered determining what is important and how to create and maintain positive momentum in your life as we do with a building project? God doesn't call us to literally do nothing, but He does call us to seek Him in the waiting. Are we first attending to what we see as urgent, or are we taking a step back to lean into what God says is truly important? No matter where we are, let's reflect and make sure that our priorities line up with those that Jesus has for us. When we do, we can experience the peace that comes from sitting at the feet of Jesus and knowing we are exactly where we're supposed to be, and the confidence in knowing our next steps are clear.

Takeaways

1. Keep the main thing as the main thing in your current season.

2. Consistently gain clarity on the difference between activity and advancement in your life.

3. Spend time with God and seek His voice to determine what He sees as advancement in your purpose for Him.

Reflections

1. What do you find urgent in your life? Make a list of everything that's screaming for your attention. Take your list to God and ask Him to help you determine what's truly important and give you clear next steps to pursue that vision.

_____

_____

_____

_____

_____

2. What main thing could you be missing right now because your focus is on what's urgent instead of important? Be honest with yourself!

_____

_____

_____

_____

_____

_____

3. What daily practice can you begin to help you keep your priorities in order (start and end, i.e., bookend, each day with reading the Bible and prayer)?

_____

_____

_____

_____

_____

_____

5

The Talking Book: Getting Ahead of God

In early 1989, I found myself wanting more personal and financial success. In my first decade in the construction business, I averaged $9,070 each year. During my second decade, I only averaged $17,000 per year. I was working long, hard hours and burning the candle at both ends, but I wasn't seeing much financial benefit. Something had to change from what I'd been doing the previous twenty years.

In 1989, a local man from my church met with me to discuss business opportunities. He had a patent on a technology that enabled printed books to be digitized and automatically read aloud. Of course, I thought this was the next big thing and became quite excited. The business had growth potential in a new market segment, ownership, and what I thought would be a significant financial upside. Carol and I invested in the company and took on the role of vice president of operations. I was also part of the team whose role was raising capital and overseeing setup and manufacturing. I was sure this was the next step I should take in a different direction.

I spent much of the year learning everything I could about this technology and what it would take to start manufacturing. I met with and pitched to major companies like Hewlett Packard and 3M, flying over 60,000 miles that year. After exhausting all our options, we settled on offshore manufacturing in Chen Zen, China.

One talent I didn't realize I had until this venture was my ability to develop and maintain relationships with investors and potential investors. Our company had raised the necessary funds to take our next steps in manufacturing. We were on the verge of securing our last big capital raise through a sophisticated investor our accountant had introduced to me. This man was on the brink of making a significant financial investment, and I could see everything coming together.

One evening, I overheard our inventor/president talking about post-funding plans for the company, which included diluting the stock, among other nefarious things. His plans would benefit him but would make it incredibly difficult for our investors to recoup their original investments, let alone see any returns.

This did not sit well with me. The focus of our inventor wasn't on building a reliable product—he was focused on making as much money as possible as quickly as possible. I struggled with this point of view and ultimately found that I could neither participate nor sit in silence. I approached the investor and my accountant and shared the company president's motives. The investor wisely backed out of the deal.

I spent much of my time during 1989 chasing something more and different, thinking it was my next step, but

it ended up as a colossal waste of my time and others' resources. As a result, I resigned from the company and visited each investor I'd recruited to share the difficult news. My dad and I were still in business at that time as well.

Recently, God has been speaking to me about the life of Moses, and I'm starting to connect the dots with parts of his life and my time back in 1989 pursuing my own goals.

> ## God prepared Moses and grew his character until he was finally ready...

Moses was born a foreigner and an enslaved person in a strange land with an unfamiliar culture, sent down a river in a basket, adopted by royalty, and raised by the Pharaoh's daughter (Exod. 2). He was a social justice advocate, a murderer, and even led an entire people to freedom. What a life!

While he did so much to advance God's kingdom during his life, I learn the most when I take a closer look at the less-than-heroic aspects of Moses's life. I chose Moses because he was not born into privilege, made the mistake of acting out of anger and murdering a man, and delayed God's plan for himself and the Israelites. I felt that my time working with the talking book was a delay in my life. He didn't start his journey as a fully equipped, successful man of God but as a baby born into captivity when Egyptians enslaved Israelites. The Pharaoh, fearing an increase in the Hebrew population and the potential for a shift in the balance of power, ordered all male Hebrew babies to be drowned in the Nile River. Moses' mother put him in a basket and sent him down the river, where he was discovered and adopted by the

Pharaoh's daughter, who raised him as her own in Pharaoh's household (Exod. 2:1-5).

Though raised as an Egyptian, Moses was troubled by how Egyptians mistreated the enslaved Israelites:

> Time passed. Moses grew up. One day he went and saw his brothers, saw all that hard labor. Then he saw an Egyptian hit a Hebrew—one of his relatives! He looked this way and then that; when he realized there was no one in sight, he killed the Egyptian and buried him in the sand. The next day he went out there again. Two Hebrew men were fighting. He spoke to the man who started it: "Why are you hitting your neighbor?" The man shot back: "Who do you think you are, telling us what to do? Are you going to kill me the way you killed that Egyptian?" Then Moses panicked: "Word's gotten out—people know about this." Pharaoh heard about it and tried to kill Moses, but Moses got away to the land of Midian. (Exod. 2:11-15 MSG)

Now, I am certainly not condoning the use of violence against someone you disagree with, but I can understand the heart behind Moses' desire for justice and the fair treatment of his people. While he may have had good intentions and compassion for his people, Moses didn't have a plan. Moses acted out of his passion to immediately right the wrong to his people but did not wait for God. I believe he should have waited not just to hear God's plan but also to know God's timing.

When Moses killed the Egyptian, he took matters into his own hands and got ahead of God. As a result, Moses fled Egypt and spent the next forty years in the desert, where God prepared Moses and grew his character until he was finally ready to return and lead the Israelites out of Egypt and into freedom. Though perhaps rooted in what he thought was just and right, Moses' zeal got him ahead of God's timing and cost an entire people thirty years of freedom from Pharaoh's bondage!

One God idea is exponentially better than chasing my own plans through my own strength.

In hindsight, which is always 20/20, I am reminded that while I was waiting on the next season of my professional life, actively desiring a change, I never stopped seeking God and pursuing His wisdom. Nothing was necessarily wrong with trying a new business venture or pursuing something I was excited about, but I let my desires take precedence. It blinded me to the fact that the company's inventor and president was using my integrity as a tool for his own financial gain.

I was asking God to bless my plans instead of asking God to show me what I should be doing and, more importantly, when I should be doing it. I learned the hard way that one God idea is exponentially better than chasing my own plans through my own strength.

It can be easy to wrongly assume that the vision or desire in our heart is from God and that He's ready to bring it to pass immediately. I can relate to Moses' zealous desire to pursue what he thought was best, but I also find comfort in the fact that God didn't allow Moses' failures and missteps to derail His plans, even if they did delay them.

> *I was asking God to bless my plans instead of asking God to show me what I should be doing.*

A few years after the talking book debacle, I crossed paths with that potential investor, and I was unsurprised to find out he'd gone on to do incredible things with his life. I learned from the investor that his unwavering faith in God has developed a rare and unwavering trust in God. The integrity move of sharing the truth with him all those years ago greatly influenced our relationship, and I doubt we'd be as close or as trusting without it. We now invest with him and have been blessed as a result.

> *To truly wait well, we must embrace what God wants us to learn, whether it matches our desires or not.*

I'm not comparing myself or any of my achievements to Moses and his, but I find comfort in knowing that even though I allowed my will to get me ahead of God's plan for my life, it was merely a delay, not a cancellation. At the time, I didn't see that I was in the middle of a storm fighting my goals and desire for success. If I had sought God's plan, I would no doubt never have pursued a stray path and would have avoided a lot of heartaches, uncomfortable conversations, and wasted time.

Fortunately, I backtracked and connected with God and His plan for my life. It took some missteps on my part, but I finally understood that God has given me unique talents and gifts and His plan and purpose is specific for my life—I just need to follow His lead or risk wandering into the desert.

Have you gotten ahead of God at some point in your life, or are you trying to go your way now? Be encouraged that God can and will still use you for His designed purposes. But you must be willing to trust His timing and ways, or you could find yourself wandering in the wilderness (and you could negatively affect those in your sphere of influence just as I did when I worked with the greedy company president and just as Moses' jumping the gun affected Israel).

Time isn't a renewable resource, and I'd rather do the right thing in God's time than waste any more of mine or anyone else's. To truly wait well, we must embrace what God wants us to learn while we wait, whether it matches our desires or not. Ask God for His timing. Remember—we may be unable to speed up God's plan, but when we take control, we can learn in the waiting season and avoid delay.

Takeaways

1. Wait on God, even when the temptation of something "better" or easier arises.

2. One God idea is exponentially better than chasing plans in our own strength.

3. Getting ahead of God may not change our destiny, but it may cause painful delays along the way.

Reflections

1. What plans do you have for your life? Have you taken them to God to see if they align with His plans for you?

_____

_____

_____

_____

_____

_____

2. Have you ever gotten ahead of God's timing? What was the result, and what did you learn from the experience?

_____

_____

_____

_____

_____

_____

3. How can you distinguish between your plans and God's plans going forward?

_____

_____

_____

_____

_____

6

Obedience in the Interim

Our daughter, Hannah Christine, was born prematurely at twenty-eight weeks and died eight days later. Those eight days at Emanuel Hospital in Portland, Oregon, were incredibly painful. Carol was convinced that the stress our young business had placed on us caused the early delivery. We later learned that it was due to a medical reason, but it didn't change how Carol felt then. One of the lowest and most difficult seasons of waiting in my life was also a time when God appeared silent.

Our doctor informed us many couples who had a child die in the Newborn Intensive Care Unit (NICU) could end up divorced. Though we were heartbroken and grieving, we did not want our marriage to be a statistic. So when Carol told me that she was not up to the stress of working in the business and no longer wanted me to work in the construction industry, I agreed.

I shifted my focus from construction to residential real estate. I was still working with homes, and it didn't seem like a giant leap. As usual, I created a plan that evaluated various options, companies, percentage splits, personalities, and company cultures and began to work on the plan. Unfortunately, I had a slow start, and any progress also came slowly. I struggled because my construction expertise allowed me to see all the faults with the properties. I stuck with it for about a year, but looking in the mirror and watching myself starve to death was a struggle. The season was incredibly lean for our family finances and a struggle for me emotionally. I didn't know what my future held, but real estate wasn't the path I'd envisioned.

I had no idea what would come next, but I knew it was important to obey God by loving Carol well and honoring her as my wife and partner in life. I was now selling real estate and not building. While I remember vividly the struggles of that year, losing a daughter and indefinitely leaving behind a career in the only field in which I felt gifted and had experience, I do not for one moment regret honoring Carol's request to put her first.

This story reminds me of the importance of obedience to God even in seasons of waiting and uncertainty. Similarly, I find comfort in God's faithfulness to Noah and his family:

> GOD saw that human evil was out of control. People thought evil, imagined evil—evil, evil, evil from morning to night. GOD was sorry that he had made the human race in the first place; it broke his heart. GOD said, "I'll get rid of my ruined creation, make a clean sweep: people, animals, snakes and bugs, birds—the works. I'm sorry I made them." But Noah was different. GOD liked what he saw in Noah. (Gen. 6:5-8 MSG)

The story of Noah and the ark is undoubtedly familiar, so I won't go over all the details. Suffice it to say, God was fed up with people and ready to start over. He was determined to wipe away humanity with a great flood, except for Noah and his family. In Noah, He saw a man of integrity, someone who could be used to rebuild the world.

The time it took Noah to build the ark and before it began to rain was 120 years. Can you imagine what the waiting must have been like? I, for one, wouldn't have been able to walk through the waiting without questioning God about whether the promised rain would ever show up. Eventually, the rain and floods came, but Noah's waiting was far from finished. Let's look at the waiting after:

- Genesis 7:12, rain was upon the earth 40 days and nights.

- Genesis 7:14, the flood was 40 days upon the earth.

- Genesis 7:24 and 8:3, waters were on the earth 150 days.

- Genesis 8:4–5, from the 17th of 2nd month to the 1st of 10th month, the waters recede while the ark was caught in the mountains. That is $(29-17) + 29 + 29 = 70$ days.

- Genesis 8:6, 40 more days and Noah opened the ark.

- Genesis 8:10, he stayed on the ark, no land yet, for another 7 days.

- Genesis 8:12, he waited another seven days, and the dove had an olive branch.

I don't even like to wait for a table at a restaurant! I often wonder how I would have felt having to wait so long preparing for the flood and then spending another 354 days cooped up on the ark. I sometimes also wonder why Noah needed to wait for anything. According to God, he walked with integrity and was about the only one doing things right: "Noah was a good man, a man of integrity in his community. Noah walked with God." (Gen. 6:9 MSG)

We all have events we don't anticipate or unexpected seasons of waiting or transition. I truly believe one of the most challenging things in life is when a parent loses a child, especially someone like Carol, who has an unlimited capacity to love. We can only connect the dots in life when we reflect on the past. When facing challenges, our faith is like our headlights when driving at night; it is dark, and we can only see as far as the lights are shining. We did not know what was next after our only daughter, Hannah, died, but we knew we needed the Lord to sustain us through the road ahead.

After we returned home and had a service and burial, we had no idea what was ahead. Carol had seven surgeries the following year from subsequent damage relating to this birth, significant medical bills were due, and they said we couldn't have any more children born to us. We were devastated.

Do you sometimes feel you're doing everything right and shouldn't have to wait either? Has God spoken to you about your future, but you have yet to see His promise fulfilled?

In Luke 3:36, Noah and his first son Shem are noted as Jesus' ancestors. I doubt Noah could have imagined that he would be an ancestor to the savior of humanity, and it makes me wonder: do any of us know how our obedience will impact not only our lives but the lives of those around us both now and in the future?

Do any of us really know how our obedience will not only impact our lives but the lives of those around us, both now and in the future?

After spending many fruitless months in real estate, Carol changed her mind and encouraged me to operate in my giftings and work in construction again. I believe my obedience in this season ultimately blessed and strengthened our marriage and enabled our business to grow and be as successful as it is today. Moreover, Carol returned fully engaged and committed as a vital part of the Desert Star team going forward, being the office manager and handling all the HR functions, client contracts, and payroll. She has the gift of being a maximizer, an asset that helped our construction company thrive, and thirty-five years later, our son Jeremy now leads as president.

The goal in any season of waiting is to trust that God has a plan more significant than our own and to follow His steps, not ours. I think it must have taken an incredible amount of courage and trust for Noah, and it will take the same from the rest of us no matter what our waiting looks like. I know God wanted to grow me in the lean seasons of real estate to prepare me for all that He had in store for the future, both in my family and business.

> *The goal (and the challenge) in any season of waiting is to trust that God has a plan bigger than our own...*

Noah was questioned, ridiculed, and laughed at. Still, he trusted that God was moving even in the waiting and chose to move forward despite challenges or circumstances or the opinions of others. (What would we think if we saw someone building what looked like a large barge in the middle of dry land with no apparent rain in the forecast?) I questioned my future while spinning my wheels in real estate when I couldn't see the next step, much less the finish line. But I chose obedience to God's ways over my comfort, which paid off more than we could have ever imagined.

To wait well, it's important to have the proper perspective. Waiting is not a burden but a blessing and an opportunity to see what God is developing if you treat it as such. Noah's time in the interim wasn't punishment but preparation. Noah's obedience in the waiting enabled Him to be used by God for such an important role.

Whether you're waiting on a relationship or your next career move, it's important to remember that, just as with Noah, God is looking for godly, obedient people He can use to change the world and make a difference in the lives of others. How will you view your waiting? How will you respond to God's call when He shows you it is time to move forward?

Takeaways

1. Lean into God's promises. Don't give up, especially when it seems to be taking much longer than you expected. Trust what God says in His Word and keep reading it aloud, telling yourself it is true. Galatians 6:9 – "Let us not grow weary or become discouraged in doing good, for at the proper time we will reap, if we do not give in."

2. The choices we make today determine who we become. This impacts the lives of those around us and our character preparedness when opportunities cross our path. Your obedience to the Lord may also impact generations to come.

3. When we are obedient to the Lord, He is faithful to always do what is best for us at the right time, bringing the right people into our lives and honoring our commitment to Him. He is faithful while we wait and will direct us when we see and get the answer to our prayers.

Reflections

1. Do you consider yourself patient? Do others? If not, how can you work toward learning and practicing patience?

_____

_____

_____

_____

_____

_____

_____

2. Has God asked you to do something where you can't see the next step or the finish line? If so, what next step of obedience can you take in the interim?

_____

_____

_____

_____

_____

_____

3. Was there a time in the past when you couldn't see what God was up to but, in hindsight, see how your obedience was part of something greater than you could have imagined? How can this encourage you in your current or future seasons of waiting?

_____

_____

_____

_____

_____

_____

_____

_____

_____

_____

_____

_____

_____

7

The Outsiders

Have you ever felt like an outsider in your season of waiting? Maybe you don't have a seat or feel like you belong at the table? Perhaps you're operating from a different playbook or even playing a different sport entirely from those around you.

I worked with and learned from an iconic architect early in my career as a general contractor. He taught me to manage client relationships by serving their needs and desires. Though DSC is a thriving company now, our beginnings were humble, as were mine. I learned to view the project from the client's perspective and never talk about other projects.

On one project, the client asked me to do something, and I said I would let her know. My mentor taught me when clients ask for something, the answer is yes. He was always available for a question about the project. Through my relationship with him, I gained a seat at the table with our clients, propelling my career to high-net-worth clients.

To say I came from a different world from our clients was true. This was the uber-wealthy sitting down at the table with me, a man who lived in a trailer, someone who was bullied as a child and at that time still carried those insecurities and feelings of inferiority.

This was a pivotal season of transition and waiting in my career. I'd just begun work as a general contractor, and I already felt out of place and out of my depth as ultra-wealthy clients surrounded me. But I was thankful for my mentor's wisdom and guidance during this season. It was time to set aside being hyper-focused on my insecurities, perceived deficiencies, or my company's needs. I realized that the best thing we could do was to go above and beyond in focusing on the needs of our clients and serving them well.

We started small by bringing lunch to long meetings so they knew we were committed to what they needed to accomplish and get the decisions we needed to keep the project moving forward. We helped create an atmosphere of comfort and productivity during meetings. We made it our mission to create a welcoming and positive environment that would leave a lasting impression on them.

We future-proofed homes for potential additions to make their lives more manageable going forward (installing conduit for fiber-optic lines, holiday lighting, etc.). We built mockups on the project site to help them envision a potential future for their designs. Every wall, water feature, pool, and driveway were identified with chalk. We also erected windows using PVC pipe to show views. Aerial images made this look like a crime scene! We even broke ground on projects with kid shovels so entire families could participate. We buried a time capsule, knowing their home would be foundational for the family's future dreams and adventures.

In short, we served our socks off and treated our clients the way we would treat family. We went above and beyond, valuing selflessness, service, and excellence. We're an industry leader with over $170,000,000 of work in progress. Looking back, it's incredible to see what God has done.

Desert Star Construction, Inc. has a registered trademark for Personal Resorts®. We have constructed the homes on parcels of land between one acre and more than 250 acres. The size (>40,000 sq. ft) and amenities set them apart from a luxury home. The projects have multiple pools, fitness rooms, salt rooms, sauna, theaters, and landscaped gardens throughout the property. We've built some of the largest Personal Resorts® for the wealthiest families in the United States, from CEOs to sports stars. If our clients all merged their companies, annual sales would exceed four trillion dollars.

We have loyal clients who entrust us with helping maintain the homes we've built for them through Desert Star Concierge®. DSC Concierge® is a proactive maintenance company that cares for homes built by our construction company and other builders, everything from handling landscaping and garage doors to appliances and chiller maintenance.

God still works in the details of everyday life, even during the times when we feel underequipped, alienated, and on the fringes.

I love the story of Ruth because she was also an outsider. Her story also has many layers to peel back and learn from. At its heart, it's a story of love and respect between two women from entirely different cultures. This revealed how God still works in the details of everyday life, even when we feel underequipped, alienated, and on the fringes. It's a story about the power of love, loyalty, and selflessness in the face of uncertainty.

During a famine in the town of Bethlehem in Israel, Naomi and her family, including her husband and two sons, traveled to the neighboring land of Moab in search of food and opportunity. Moab had a completely different culture from Israel, worshipping its own gods.

After their arrival, Naomi's husband died. Her sons, who had both married Moabite women, also died. This left Naomi a stranger in a strange land with two foreign daughters-in-law, Ruth and Orpah. Naomi, resigned to her difficult circumstances, encouraged her two daughters-in-law to stay in their native home while she returned to Bethlehem widowed and alone. Orpah agreed to stay, but Ruth made a decision that undoubtedly shocked Naomi:

> But Ruth said, "Don't force me to leave you; don't make me go home. Where you go, I go; and where you live, I'll live. Your people are my people, your God is my god; where you die, I'll die, and that's where I'll be buried, so help me GOD—not even death itself is going to come between us!" (Ruth 1:16-17 MSG)

Ruth made the unprecedented commitment to Naomi to follow her and support her wherever she went. She was grieving the sudden death of her husband, just as Naomi was mourning the death of her husband, followed by the death of her two sons—her entire family. I doubt choosing to leave everything and everyone she's ever known to travel to a foreign country with a completely different culture, customs, and values was easy. But Ruth loved Naomi, valued their relationship, and made the unwavering commitment to choose faith in God and obedience to His ways to support Naomi. Despite this, Naomi had nothing of tangible value to offer Ruth, nor could Naomi have more sons.

I can't imagine what was happening inside Ruth during her journey. She was likely the focus of gossip when she arrived with Naomi as a Gentile outsider in Bethlehem and among the widows. She would have been viewed as a second-class citizen by the Israelites there. At one point in her life, she felt that she had everything, and now she had nothing and was afflicted by God.

> "Don't call me Naomi," she told them. "Call me Mara, because the Almighty has made my life very bitter. I went away full, but the LORD has brought me back empty. Why call me Naomi? The LORD has afflicted me; the Almighty has brought misfortune upon me."
> (Ruth 1:20-21 NIV)

I doubt Ruth could have imagined what God had in store for her. Her husband was gone, and she was in a new place. But this did not deter her from waiting with integrity and a servant's heart. Ruth went out of her way to honor and help provide for her mother-in-law, gathering leftovers from the harvest fields. Ruth sought to serve others in her season of waiting, which prepared the way for God to do something incredible during that time.

Ruth met Boaz, a close relative of Naomi's family and the owner of the harvest field where she gathered barley. In the Jewish culture, it was the duty of the closest relative to redeem a widowed woman by marrying, caring for, and extending her family line. Boaz was the redeemer for Naomi's family. Boaz made a big impression on Ruth through his kindness to her, who then shared the story with Naomi. Naomi encouraged Ruth to seek him out. In response, Ruth acts with tremendous boldness as she follows Naomi's suggestions, placing herself in the presence of Boaz and even proposing to him.

Throughout the remainder of the story, Ruth and Boaz interact with a mutual degree of honor and respect, culminating in Boaz marrying Ruth and redeeming Naomi's family. Ruth and Boaz clearly had immense respect for each other and love for God. Their obedience was part of God's plan from the beginning, as was Ruth's love, loyalty, and servant's heart.

Ruth then gave birth to Obed, grandfather of King David in the lineage of Jesus Christ (Matt. 1:1-17). Ruth chose to leave the comfort of her culture, follow God, and pursue His ways by loving and caring for Naomi. As a result, she became a generational grandmother to the Savior of humanity! God was clearly at work in the details of this story, and He used Ruth's selflessness to bless her and prepare the way for an essential part of the story of Jesus.

We can learn so much from Ruth, someone I'm sure felt ill-equipped during her season of waiting in a foreign territory. She trusted Naomi's wisdom and guidance, resulting in a beautiful story of redemption and blessing. I often wonder about businesses that ignore their clients' or customers' wisdom and guidance and refuse to adapt. Could they have done better in business if they had listened to others?

Ruth was also an incredible example of how we can wait during our seasons of uncertainty—by focusing on and serving others. Though I was outside of the world I was comfortable in and didn't know what to expect, I chose to serve all our clients with integrity.

We have a tradition of feeding everyone who works on a Desert Star Project. Every month, we purchase lunch for the unsung heroes of our projects who often work long, hard hours in the summer heat, doing anything to get the job done right. Attendees range from field superintendents and project executives to project managers and project engineers. We've done everything from catering simple lunches to hosting full Thanksgiving and Christmas dinners. It's a small token of generosity to communicate our gratitude.

Don't know what to do? Feel like you're on foreign ground? Honor God by serving those around you and watch Him move in ways you could never imagine.

What we do for our team was reinforced when I attended dinner with a client. We have clients from across the world, and most are at the top of their industry or field. We had completed a complex hillside, multimillion-dollar renovation in every area of their home for this client we were dining with. For this dinner, the attendees were the client's Board of Directors, and they flew in from around the world.

(Why was I even there?) These dinner guests included the head of a stock exchange, university law professors, and others with doctorates in physics, biology, history, and more. Most of those at the table were highly educated and graciously spoke English for my benefit—it would have been a long evening if they hadn't.

Our dinner was served at sunset on the outside patio of the completed residence. We sat across the table from our client, with his pilot to my left and the sommelier to my right. The client made a dish from his native Switzerland and then served the two flight attendants, the pilot, the sommelier, and then me. I asked why he served in this order, and his answer was simple and impactful. He said, "In our country, we serve first those who serve us."

I'm not saying our client focus resulted in something as beautiful as the redemption of a family or as important as establishing a family line that includes Jesus. But the story of Ruth reminds me of the blessings found in adding value to others despite our position, circumstances, or season of life.

Desert Star is no doubt where we are now because we decided to focus on adding value to others even when we didn't feel qualified to be sitting at the same table as them. I am also encouraged that God is still involved in the details. He's just as interested in our lives as He was in Ruth's, and He's working just the same on our behalf.

Regardless of what we are waiting on or whether we have any idea of what's next, we can choose to wait with integrity and selflessly serve others. This is a way to bless God's heart and should be the default for our waiting times as God grows our character and prepares us for what's ahead. Do you feel like you're in foreign territory and do not have a seat at your desired table? Don't know what to do? Honor

God by serving those around you and watch Him move in ways you could never imagine.

Takeaways

1. Choose to serve others to the best of your ability during your season of waiting.

2. Stay focused on serving others even when you feel ill-equipped or inadequate.

3. Not only will you bless others by serving them well, but you will be blessed in ways you can't yet imagine.

Reflections

1. Have you ever felt ill-equipped during your season of transition or waiting? Did you ask God for direction or clarity? Did you wait or move ahead with your own plan? How did you respond in the moment, and what effect did your response have in the long term?

_____

_____

_____

_____

_____

2. How do you respond when people put you ahead of themselves? How can you do the same for those around you?

_____

_____

_____

_____

_____

_____

3. How can you lead those around you or under your leadership to selflessly serve others in your sphere of influence professionally and personally? How can you lead your family, friends, business associates, and new relationships?

_____

_____

_____

_____

_____

_____

8

When Silence Is Deafening

While I've often heard from God and been convinced of my next steps, just as many times, no matter how hard I press into Him or seek His wisdom, I don't get the immediate response I'm searching for. It's frustrating but also an opportunity to grow my patience and learn what God wants from me in the silence.

In 2008, DSC faced an incredible amount of uncertainty through the recession and the bursting of the real estate bubble. Projects were drying up, and we didn't know from where they'd come next. We had $27,000,000 of work canceled or postponed, a business dependent upon a tanking market, and I had no idea what we would do. God had not given me a clear five-step plan on how we could survive, much less thrive, amidst the economic recession.

> *I boldly stated that we were not going to participate in the recession, that we work in God's economy and our objective was to grow, not to shrink.*

It was easy to get frustrated by circumstances and a lack of clear next steps. But during this time, I became increasingly grateful for God's people in my life—the successful people at Desert Star we invested in and the people who mattered. While I didn't know what to do, I knew the answer wasn't to cut back and lay off the same people who helped build and grow Desert Star. There was no way I would cut them loose simply because the world was in chaos. Our people make the difference, and I was going to have their backs.

When everything stopped, we gathered our team, and I boldly stated that we would not participate in the recession, that we work in God's economy, and that our objective was to grow, not shrink. Amazingly, we worked through the financial collapse of 2008 without laying off any of our team. We were among the blessed few starting large, new projects.

What does this story have to do with waiting? I share it because of something that hit me while reading Psalm 77 by King David.

We could read an entire series of books learning from David's relationship with God: *Great Lives: David* by Charles Swindoll, *David the Great*, Mark Rutland; *The Making of a Man of God* by Alan Redpath, and most important . . . the book of Psalms in the Bible. The Bible recounts his early, faith-filled days as a shepherd to defeating Goliath and rescuing Israel to being crowned king of Israel after Saul. While David was successful, he was not exempt from failure, making him much more relatable. His tragic failures see him humbled and his kingdom destroyed. David's emotionally honest Psalms reflect his relationship with God and a deep desire for His ways despite David's many shortcomings. This is why, despite his failures, David is re-membered as a man after God's own heart (1 Sam. 13:14, Acts 13:22).

In Psalm 77, David, King over all of Israel and favored by God, wrestled with and questioned God and received no answer. Even though he had no idea how he'd make it through, David prayed:

> I cried out to God for help;
>   I cried out to God to hear me.
> When I was in distress, I sought the Lord;
>   at night I stretched out untiring hands,
>   and I would not be comforted...
> "Will the Lord reject forever?
>   Will he never show his favor again?
> Has his unfailing love vanished forever?
>   Has his promise failed for all time?
> Has God forgotten to be merciful?
>   Has he in anger withheld his compassion?"
> (Ps. 77:1-2, 7-9 NIV)

Whether David was surrounded by external enemies or reaping self-inflicted emotional destruction at the time of writing this psalm, he didn't stay in the valley of despair for long. Mid-psalm, he shifted his focus to remembering all the good things God had already done in his life, all the reasons he had to rejoice:

> Then I thought, "To this I will appeal:
>   the years when the Most High stretched out
>   his right hand.

I will remember the deeds of the Lord;
 yes, I will remember your miracles of long
 ago.
I will consider all your works
 and meditate on all your mighty deeds."
(Ps. 77:10-12 NIV)

This struck a chord with me. As mentioned, I am not the most patient person in the world. I prefer to have a plan and work it as quickly and effectively as possible. Inactivity pains me, and I certainly don't enjoy sitting in silence when it comes to hearing from God about my next steps. I was confident we would get through the economic crisis if I trusted God. Keeping the team together was the priority, but we also made use of the time: We went through every process and simplified it, and we started investing in our team's education, training, and valuing their families and our trade partners.

But I found comfort in David's response and something I could model in my life. I realized that it's OK not to have a clue about what God is up to, and it's OK to have moments of doubt. But what wasn't helpful for David, and I've found is never beneficial for me, is camping out in a place of doubt and despair. In shifting his focus to all the good God had done in his life, David changed his perspective and showed true faith.

His attitude set the stage for God to do a mighty work of redemption in David. When we choose gratitude during God's silence, we can set the stage for Him to do a powerful work in and through us.

> *When we choose gratitude during God's silence, we can set the stage for Him to do a mighty work in and through us as well.*

In the fourth quarter of 2015, Desert Star was finishing thirteen projects, but for some reason, we couldn't sign a new project or, in many cases, even get a face-to-face meeting with clients, and those that we did meet never selected us. We couldn't get a single project to go our way. We were chasing down every lead and project we could think of. I prayed for clarity and answers, but God remained quiet.

During this season, I started putting into practice what I learned from David in Psalm 77. I still had no idea how we were to move forward, but I reflected on all the ways God had been faithful in the past, personally and professionally. This went against my natural tendency to solve problems and plow forward in my strength!

I was thankful for my beautiful wife and children, Jeremy and Jonathan. My work family. The roof over my head. The shoes on my feet. The fact that I had a job at all, much less one that allowed me to pursue my passions and use my God-given talents to make a difference in the lives of others. Whether large or small, I thought about all the good things God had done in my life. Even at Desert Star, we hadn't just survived the 2008 recession—God had helped us grow and thrive amid economic collapse. He'd been faithful in the past and could certainly do it again.

> *While it can be easy to see God's silence as a roadblock or an obstacle to overcome, I encourage you to shift your perspective and view it as an opportunity to slow down and take stock of all that you have to be grateful for.*

In early October of the same year, I received a call from an architect with whom we'd never previously worked. He was vacationing in Bora Bora and reading my first book, *The Teambuilder Toolbox (TBT),* written in 2015. TBT was the response to people in our industry wanting to know why we were so successful; my answer was always thank you, but it was one thousand of my closest friends and me. He said he needed us to fast-track a project I wrote about in the book and wanted to meet the following Monday. Even though we needed the work, I didn't want to appear anxious, so I told him I would check my schedule and get back to him.

What came about was exceedingly and abundantly more than we could have imagined. Though I can't share the whole story due to confidentiality agreements, the result was monumental. We signed contracts for not one but two significant personal resorts within two days of each other. Both projects were multi-year in duration, among some of the largest homes ever built in Arizona (and America).

> *Even at Desert Star, we hadn't just survived the 2008 recession—God had helped us to grow and thrive in the midst of economic collapse.*

The funny thing is that both projects had different architects; this was the first time we'd worked with either architectural firm. We didn't know the clients, and as far as we knew, they had never stepped foot in one of our Personal Resorts®. We would never have had the time or resources to work on either of these projects if we were awarded any of the previous projects we'd been so disappointed to lose out on.

I recall later showing one of the clients through a completed project to look at the window systems and various finishes. I was literally on my knees explaining the artisanal details about the reclaimed wood floors and where to see the detailed work involved at the terminations of the different materials. I stopped mid-explanation and asked the client why I was still selling since we already had the job. We all laughed, and the client asked me to continue.

At that moment, it finally set in that I was in the middle of a miracle, a true blessing from God. I left the meeting with tears streaming down my face as I realized how blessed we were and how good God was. I pulled over on the side of the road and called Carol to share.

> *The quiet can be a blessing,*
> *a chance to allow God's past*
> *faithfulness to sustain you, draw*
> *you closer to Him, and prepare*
> *you for the purposes and*
> *plans He has for you—don't*
> *miss the opportunity!*

What happened in 2008 and 2015 was remarkable. While I may have had no clue about what came next in those seasons, God knew what He was doing. While waiting in silence and learning the value of gratitude, God was laying the foundations of this new season for my family and business.

While it can be easy to see God's silence as a roadblock or an obstacle to overcome, I encourage you to shift your perspective. View it as an opportunity to slow down and take stock of all you have to be grateful for. The quiet can be a blessing, a chance to allow God's past faithfulness to sustain you, draw you closer to Him, and prepare you for the purposes and plans He has for you—don't miss the opportunity!

Takeaways

1. Count every blessing during your waiting seasons—you will be surprised at how blessed you already are.

2. When you don't hear from God, trust that He is still with you, for you, and preparing the way.

3. Reflect on God's past faithfulness to you and continue to thank Him for all He has done and is doing in your life.

Reflections

1. Think of a season when you weren't sure of your next step and God's plan wasn't clear. What was the outcome? How did you respond in the moment?

_____

_____

_____

_____

_____

_____

_____

2. If you are having a hard time trying to think of what you are grateful for, start with sunshine and oxygen. Regardless of what season you are in now, what are five things you are grateful for? Include your family, friends, or anything good.

_____

_____

_____

_____

_____

3. How can you daily cultivate an attitude of gratitude (writing down blessings, helping someone less fortunate, thanking people regularly)?

_____

_____

_____

_____

_____

_____

9

A Matter of Persistence

In 1997, DSC was doing well financially and internally with our team culture. We had two projects under construction at the same time, both with budgets around $3 million. (This was light years beyond where we'd only recently sat after finishing our first project of over one million dollars.) Business was good. Life was good.

In our market, many commercial construction giants saw the custom luxury residential market solely as an opportunity for financial gain. Rarely did they share our passion for the work and serving clients with excellence. For our team at Desert Star, this was the main thing, not just another business opportunity. Competition became fierce in the 1990s, and we knew it was only a matter of time before seeing a well-established, well-funded competitor appear. That moment arrived in the spring of 1997.

We interviewed for a large, custom residence in Paradise Valley, Arizona. During the bidding process, we rarely know who or when other contractors are being interviewed for the same project. But when I saw another truck upon my arrival and a different one while I was leaving, I knew we'd seen the arrival of well-established and well-funded competitors. Our first competitor was well on its way to being a billion-dollar business. The other was doing slightly over $150 million. At this point, we were working on $5 million in total annual revenue. It was our David versus Goliath moment, and I was determined that it would not matter how big our competition was. The values of our team and the size of my God would trump anything we faced.

The values of our team and the size of my God would trump anything we faced.

I was confident that I did my best in the interview, and a few weeks later, the architect told me they were leaning toward our small company. Several weeks passed, and I hadn't heard from the client. In June of 1997, I reached out to the client, who made it clear he appreciated our efforts, but he and his wife wouldn't make a final decision until the end of the year. More waiting.

The silence and waiting drove me a little crazy, but in hindsight, I know that this is where God was growing me. At times in my past, I would have tried to push forward and make my way. Typically, I would contact everyone I knew associated with the client and ask for support, consistently follow up with the architect who introduced me to the client, and reach out to the client weekly. God was at work within me, and I believed He was preparing me for a crucial moment of boldness to take a step through a door only He could open.

> *While we may not always know exactly what our next step is, God doesn't call us to sit idly by and do nothing. In our stillness, we can choose to trust God and pursue His ways actively.*

It can be easy to get ahead of God while we wait, carving out our path and plotting a course we think will help us take our next steps to get us to where we think we're supposed to be. We've seen Moses' attempt to expedite God's timeline and the disastrous results, including an extended time in the wilderness and delaying God's plan for an entire nation by thirty years (Gen. 15:13 = 400 years; Exod. 12:40 = 430 years).

The Bible has countless examples of God asking us to trust and wait on Him. Notably, in Exodus 14:14, Moses says, "The Lord will fight for you; you only need to be still" (NIV). I can't tell you how often I've seen this verse referenced about waiting. But I've also found it can be just as easy to sit in idleness, waiting for a movement from God to create the change we hope to see. But I don't think God was calling Moses to do nothing. Instead, He was calling Moses to put His trust in God and stop trying to control the outcome of everything through his strength. In short, trust God and follow His ways, and the rest will work itself out.

While we may not always know exactly what our next step is, God doesn't call us to sit idly by and do nothing. In our stillness, we can choose to actively trust God and pursue His ways.

In Luke 18:1-8, Jesus shared with His disciples the Parable of the Persistent Widow, and we can learn a lot about persistence in prayer from this brief story:

> Then Jesus told his disciples a parable to show them that they should always pray and not give up. He said: "In a certain town there was a judge who neither feared God nor cared what people thought. And there was a widow in that town who kept coming to him with the plea, 'Grant me justice against my adversary.'
>
> "For some time he refused. But finally he said to himself, 'Even though I don't fear God or care what people think, yet because this widow keeps bothering me, I will see that she gets justice, so that she won't eventually come and attack me!'"
>
> And the Lord said, "Listen to what the unjust judge says. And will not God bring about justice for his chosen ones, who cry out to him day and night? Will he keep putting them off? I tell you, he will see that they get justice, and quickly. However, when the Son of Man comes, will he find faith on the earth?" (NIV)

While on the surface the story is about pursuing justice, it is intended to encourage us to seek God in prayer persistently. But as I read the parable, I can't help but think that God also calls us to trust Him and be persistent in how we pursue ALL His ways and what He's placed on our hearts. The widow knew that God is just, clung to the truth, and was persistent in her pursuit of His ways. I believe God desires similar persistence from us even today.

Fast-forward to 8:00 p.m. on New Year's Eve, 1997. I knew God had brought me into a relationship with this client for a reason, but it would require a moment of boldness to take the next step. Through some creative detective work, I found out where our client would be spending New Year's Eve and obtained the phone number to their vacation home.

> *I knew God had brought me into a relationship with this client for a reason, but it would require a moment of boldness to take the next step.*

Though a bit fearful and insecure, I picked up the phone and dialed. The client answered, and I wished him a happy new year after I identified myself. I reminded him that he'd told me he would decide on his builder by the end of the year. I told him I didn't want to interrupt him later in the evening but wanted to know their decision.

While I think the client was a bit shocked, he said that he and his wife wanted Desert Star to build their new home. Little did I know that this was the beginning of a great friendship and a professional relationship. This project was also the catalyst for the exponential growth of our company over the next twenty years.

In the parable, the persistent widow could have accepted the judge's first response and left downcast and defeated. Still, she recognized that God had brought her to the threshold of something and that He would honor her persistence—so she boldly went after it. I'm not saying the parable is identical to when I pursued our client to ensure he kept his word. But God placed it on my heart to pursue that opportunity with integrity.

I absolutely believe He was waiting to see what I'd do in response.

He opened a door and brought me to the threshold, and I absolutely believe He was waiting to see what I'd do in response. To see if I would trust him enough to step through the open door to which He'd brought me. In the end, there was no way I wouldn't be persistent in my pursuit of something God so clearly put on my heart.

While not every good opportunity is necessarily an open door from God, I firmly believe that God wants us to go after His ways and be persistent in our pursuit of Him regardless of where we find ourselves. Just as He did with so many heroes of the faith in biblical times, God still brings us to the doorstep of opportunity.

But how do we respond? Do we sit idly by and wait for God? Have we considered that He may simply be watching and waiting for us to show our faith in Him by boldly stepping into His calling on our lives?

> *To be persistent in the right things (God's ways), we must have faith that God is who He says He is and that what He's told us and put on our hearts is true and worthy of pursuit.*

DSC was successful in 1997. But after facing off against our giants in two commercial competitors and persistently pursuing the opportunity God put in front of us, our company achieved a growth and influence I could never have dreamed of. We could say it's our hard work, but I genuinely believe it's because we've boldly and persistently pursued the path God put before us.

I believe persistence and faith are two sides of the same coin that go hand in hand. To be persistent in the right things (God's ways), we must have faith that God is who He says He is and that what He's told us and put on our hearts is true and worthy of pursuit.

What door has God opened for you? What's stopping you from walking through it? Cast fear and self-doubt aside and be persistent in pursuing God's calling on your life. If you're committed to God's ways along the way, you'll never be in danger of missing His will for your life.

Takeaways

1. Waiting doesn't mean remaining idle—it's an opportunity to trust God and pursue His ways.

2. God will open doors and lead you forward, but He also wants you to be bold and take active steps forward in faith.

3. Be persistent in God's ways; He will honor your prayers and show you what is possible with Him.

Reflections

1. What vision has God put on your heart for every area of your life?

_____

_____

_____

_____

_____

_____

2. Are you currently waiting on God? Have you considered that maybe God is waiting for a moment of action on your part?

_____

_____

_____

_____

_____

_____

3. How can you be boldly in pursuit of the vision God has given you (start a vision board, write down your goals, network with others who can help your vision)? Ask Him, listen, and act!

_____

_____

_____

_____

_____

10

Risk, Uncertainty, and Reward

In the April 2009 issue of *The New Yorker*, James Surowiecki, who wrote *The New Yorker*'s financial page from 2000 to 2017, authored an interesting story about Kellogg and Post in his article, "Hanging Tough." In the late 1920s, these two companies dominated the relatively new market for packaged cereal. Ready-to-eat cereal had been around for decades, but Americans didn't see it as a real alternative to oatmeal or cream of wheat until the twenties. When the Great Depression hit, no one knew what would happen to consumer demand.

Post did the predictable thing, reined in expenses, and cut back on advertising. On the other hand, Kellogg doubled its ad budget, moved into radio advertising, and heavily pushed its new cereal, Rice Krispies. (Snap, Crackle, and Pop first appeared in the thirties.)

By 1933, even as the economy cratered, Kellogg's profits had risen almost 30%, becoming what it remains today: the industry's dominant player. For the year ending June 30,

2021, Post's annual revenue was $6,227,000,000, and Kellogg's was more than double at $14,181,000,000. The bold move of playing to win is still paying off.

You would think that everyone would want to emulate Kellogg's success, but when hard times hit, most companies end up acting more like Post. They hunker down, cut spending, and wait for the good times to return. They make fewer acquisitions, even though prices are lower. They cut advertising budgets and often invest less in research and development. They do all this to preserve what they have. But there's a trade-off: numerous studies have shown that companies that keep spending on the acquisition, advertising, and research and development during recessions do significantly better than those that make big cuts.

An advertising study during the 1981-82 recession found that sales at firms that increased advertising or held steady grew precipitously in the next three years, compared with only slight increases at firms that had slashed their budgets. A 1990-91 recession study found that companies that remained market leaders or became serious challengers during the downturn had increased their acquisition, research and development, and ad budgets, while companies at the bottom of the pile had reduced them.

One way to read these studies is recessions make the strong stronger and the weak weaker since the strong can afford to keep investing while the weak must devote all their energies to staying afloat.

When times are good and everyone is advertising, separating yourself from the pack isn't easy. When ads are scarcer, the returns on investment seem to rise. That may be why twice as many companies leaped from the bottom of their industries to the top before and after the 1990-91 recession. Although deep pockets help in a downturn, recessions still create more opportunities for challengers, not less.

Why are some companies so quick to cut back when trouble hits? The answer has to do with a famous distinction that the economist Frank Knight made between risk and uncertainty. Risk describes a situation where you have a sense of the range and likelihood of possible outcomes. Uncertainty describes a situation where it's not even clear what might happen, let alone how likely the possible outcomes are.

Uncertainty indeed creates an opportunity for serious profits, and history is full of companies that made successful gambles in hard times. In 1933, Kraft introduced Miracle Whip in six months and saw it become America's best-selling dressing. Texas Instruments brought out the transistor radio during the 1954 recession. Apple launched the iPod in 2001. But history is also filled with forgotten companies that gambled and failed (Surowiecki).

We live in a season of life that is full of disruption. Changes have caused some companies to close while others have adapted and grown stronger. Big box stores like Wal-Mart, Lowes, Home Depot, and others changed how we do business. Starbucks came on the scene, creating fresh and inviting spaces for people to connect, and have impacted many local coffee shops. Uber changed how we think about and use transportation. Does anyone even remember Blockbuster Video? All this before we even mention the disruption of COVID-19.

> *If we aren't open to growing and learning during whatever season we're in, we'll miss out on the big plans we had or get left behind altogether. It's not the strong who survive, it's the adaptable.*

The academics Peter Dickson and Joseph Giglierano have argued that companies must worry about two kinds of failure: "sinking the boat" (wrecking the company by making a bad bet) or "missing the boat" (letting a great opportunity pass) (Surowiecki). Today, most companies are far more worried about sinking the boat than missing it.

As with anything, perspective is essential. Uber didn't doom the cab companies; the cab companies refused to change. Many local shops went out of business not because of Starbucks but because they didn't adapt. Blockbuster didn't take advantage of the enormous opportunity the internet and streaming provided.

In the season of COVID-19, I have observed that the unprepared are usually in survival mode, while the adaptable are constantly seeking to reinvent—it's a mindset.

> *Today, most companies are far more worried about sinking the boat than about missing it.*

What will people say about you and me, your company, church, or organization when they reflect on the disruptive season of COVID-19? How we look at disruptions and times of risk, uncertainty, and waiting is essential. If we aren't open to growing and learning during whatever season we're in, we'll miss out on the big plans we had or get left behind altogether. It's not the strong who survive, it's the adaptable.

Playing not to lose reminds me of my early days when fear and insecurity seemed to guide me. Playing not to lose is Jonah running from God, or when I could continue making $17,000 per year instead of pushing through my fear and insecurity when I did not have a "seat at the table." Playing not to lose was about hanging onto what little I had. Fear caused me to be overly cautious when action was needed, which is when my dad taught me about "doing it afraid."

In 2008, as president, I consciously decided our company would not participate in the recession. Rather than dwelling on the current economy, we focused on everything good about our clients and team. I wanted to operate in God's economy.

When I think about God's economy, I realize that eleven of Jesus' thirty-nine parables spoke about money. Money is mentioned more than 800 times in the New Testament. His word governs God's economy. The system on earth requires an exchange of cash for products and services. God's economy is about sowing and reaping and the power of blessing. A few verses that helped me understand this concept:

The earth belongs to God! Everything in all the world is his! (Ps. 24:1 TLB)

Always remember that it is the Lord your God who gives you power to become rich, and he does it to fulfill his promise to your ancestors. (Deut. 8:18 TLB)

Don't be obsessed with getting more material things. Be relaxed with what you have. Since God assured us, "I'll never let you down, never walk off and leave you," we can boldly quote, God is there, ready to help; I'm fearless no matter what. Who or what can get to me? (Heb. 13:5-6 MSG)

There comes a time in our life when we stop trusting in our financial strength and begin trusting God for what is possible.

> *"In God's economy, nothing is wasted. Through failure, we learn a lesson in humility which is probably needed, painful though it is."*
> *— Bill W.*

Additionally, we were keenly aware that we also had the best clients in our community. Rather than wait to see what happened, we created a plan to review and improve our entire organization and everything we did from beginning to end. We focused on what we could do to continue our growth and the opportunity around us, a glut of homes for sale.

Most of these homes were not worth much, but their land had value. We approached clients through their realtors and recommended we salvage their house. People could imagine their home on a blank canvas with a wide-open lot. The company we worked with provided appraisals and salvaged all materials. The tax deductions received by clients ranged from the low hundreds of thousands to millions of dollars. Rather than sticking with building new, we pivoted 180 degrees, and I became Demolition Man. After DSC contacted the real estate agents in Paradise Valley, Arizona, they embraced the benefit of receiving a tax deduction for their home, salvaging, donating, recycling materials, and demolishing the remaining house.

As we draw near the end of our time together, I'd like to impart something that has consistently made a difference in my life and business: I always play to win instead of not to lose. Previously in this chapter, we addressed playing not to lose. Playing to win was Kellogg's bold move to invest in their company, which yielded positive results that more than doubled their sales to $14,181,000,000. For our company, it was when we decided to invest in our team and continue paying them until the economy turned around.

At DSC, we've faced countless seasons of disruption. We chose to bet on ourselves and our company, and I am confident that our choices in times of uncertainty are why we are at the top of our industry today. We bet on ourselves by focusing on the Lord by praying (Phil. 4:6), applying what King Solomon wrote about detailed and diligent planning in Proverbs 21:5, and reminding ourselves that God wants to give us a future and hope (Jer. 29:11).

The plans of the diligent lead surely to plenty,
but those of everyone who is hasty, surely to
poverty. (Prov. 21:5 NKJV)

Trusting God is the best way to bet on yourself. It is
total dependence on Him, and He is the first person we
should go to when we need clarity in the unknown.

Trust GOD from the bottom of your heart;
don't try to figure out everything on your own.
Listen for GOD's voice in everything you do,
everywhere you go; he's the one who will keep
you on track. (Prov. 3:5-6 MSG)

Are you more concerned with playing not to lose or
playing to win? Ask God what you can learn and who you
can become during this season of waiting—you'll find yourself with a head start in accomplishing more than you can
imagine.

Takeaways

1. When challenges come, invest in your team and look for positive opportunities in your marketplace, both internally and externally.

2. It is not the strong that survive. It is the adaptable.

3. Play to win—don't play to avoid losing.

Reflections

1. What disruptions or uncertainty are you currently facing?

_____

_____

_____

_____

_____

_____

_____

2. How can you adapt to grow in whatever season you find yourself? Ask God for the wisdom to learn from this time.

_____

_____

_____

_____

_____

_____

_____

3. What does playing to win look like for you right now? How can you play to win instead of not to lose?

_____

_____

_____

_____

_____

_____

_____

11

Burn Your Ships

Alexander the Great is widely considered one of the most outstanding military leaders the world has ever known. When he landed his military on the shores of Persia in 334 BCE, he immediately ordered them to burn the ships they'd arrived on, eliminating any possibility or even thought of retreat.

Alexander ruled over the largest empire the world had ever seen, and he knew the value of proper motivation. We still hear the phrase "Burn your ships" or "Burn your boats," which speaks to its timeless nature. Though it's more likely to be heard in a business or personal leadership setting today, the sentiment remains the same as over 2,000 years ago: there's no turning back; the only option is forward. Alexander told his men, "We will either return home in Persian ships or we will die here."

There's no turning back; the only option is forward.

As Christians, we aren't daily seeking to expand a worldly empire or acquire more resources like Alexander or so many others in history. But whether we choose to acknowledge it or not, we are in the middle of a daily spiritual battle. Alexander The Great learned from what was behind him and was unwilling to accept defeat. He learned from his past and was willing to burn the ships so he would never return. He fought for the future, and we should take the same approach with our lives. Forget the negative things from our past and press on toward the future God wants us to possess. The Apostle Peter wrote about just how clear the danger is:

> Be alert and of sober mind. Your enemy the devil prowls around like a roaring lion looking for someone to devour. Resist him, standing firm in the faith, because you know that the family of believers throughout the world is undergoing the same kind of sufferings.
> (1 Pet. 5:8-9 NIV)

The Apostle Paul also reminded us that we are called to be fighters.

> The weapons we fight with are not the weapons of the world. On the contrary, they have divine power to demolish strongholds. We demolish arguments and every pretension that sets itself up against the knowledge of God, and we take captive every thought to make it obedient to Christ. (2 Cor. 10:4-5 NIV)

The primary battle that I see is in our minds. We may not actively be engaging in warfare or battle in the worldly, traditional sense of the word, but we are called to take territory from the enemy and expand God's kingdom on earth. Focusing on yesterday's failures—am I good enough, am I worthy of God's love—keeps us focused on yesterday. By leaving the past in the past, the focus changes from who we were to who we can become.

I've never served in the military, but I agree with Alexander and many leaders throughout history—you can't effectively fight with one eye focused on your avenue of retreat.

We are reminded of the same thought by the words of Jesus in Luke 9:62: Jesus replied, "No one who puts a hand to the plow and looks back is fit for service in the kingdom of God" (NIV). In Matthew 6:24, Jesus said, "No one can serve two masters, for either he will hate the one and love the other, or he will be devoted to the one and despise the other" (NIV).

> ## You can't effectively fight with one eye focused on your avenue of retreat.

Whether we like it or not, if we choose to follow Christ, we choose a life of persecution. Google defines persecution as "hostility and ill-treatment, especially because of race or political or religious beliefs."

> In fact, everyone who wants to live a godly life in Christ Jesus will be persecuted, while evildoers and impostors will go from bad to worse, deceiving and being deceived. But as for you,

continue in what you have learned and have become convinced of, because you know those from whom you learned it... (2 Tim. 3:12 NIV)

This chapter is Scripture-heavy because I want to stress the seriousness of God's calling. Of course, our journeys will look different; God has made each of us unique with different giftings and talents. But we all share that we will face persecution and opportunities to succumb to the world's standards. We are all impacted by what has happened in our past. What will we do today within our current situation and place on our journey? My construction journey has given me a unique perspective in many areas. For example, we can entirely demolish a large house in a day, but it would take a year to build it. It is always easier to tear something down than to build it up. Stop tearing yourself down by dwelling on your past. Be resilient, disciplined, focused, and work hard for your better future. Jesus did not ask His disciples to burn their boats, but he did ask them to leave them behind. Burning your ships or leaving your boats behind is about commitment and dedication.

If we are to successfully run our race and fight the good fight (2 Tim. 4:7-8), we can't do so with one foot in the world and one foot in God's ways. We can't be successful if we keep one eye on the future and one on our means of retreat. We must burn our ships and move forward, entirely focused on pursuing all God has for us.

What occurs when we burn our ships and press forward with God? Yes, we face persecution, but we also have the incredible opportunity to take ground for God's Kingdom and to develop and walk daily in the power of the Fruit of the Holy Spirit:

But what is transformed when we live God's way? He brings gifts into our lives, much the way fruit appears in an orchard—things like affection for others, exuberance about life, and serenity. We develop a willingness to stick with things, a sense of compassion in the heart, and a conviction that a basic holiness permeates things and people. We find ourselves involved in loyal commitments, not needing to force our way in life, and able to marshal and direct our energies wisely (Gal. 5:22-23 MSG).

> *We can't be successful if we keep one eye on the future and one on our means of retreat. We must burn our ships and move forward fully focused on pursuing all that God has for us.*

I heard many messages about the Fruit of the Spirit during my youth. The idea that although God gives us gifts, fruit is grown stuck with me. The Fruit of the Spirit isn't just given but grown in due season as we step into and walk in all that God has for us. Walking through the produce aisle makes it easy to get what I want and take it home; they are fully grown. For the farmer to grow fruit, in most cases, he plants seeds and waters, keeps the weeds out, and harvests the fully matured fruit. There are seasons for the fruit and seasons for each of us. We need to grow the fruits God gave us. Work on keeping the weeds out. A harvest will come in the right season of your life. What patience I have, I've earned through many seasons that God has pruned me and refined me.

> *What happens when we burn our ships and press forward with God? Yes, we face persecution, but we also have the incredible opportunity to take ground for God's Kingdom and to develop and walk daily in the power of the Fruit of the Holy Spirit.*

And let's not forget that refinement doesn't happen without a refining fire. We want the fruits that come through improvement, but how many of us are willing to walk through the fire and allow God to change us?

While we may ask for patience, we are rarely just given a supernatural grace for others; we are given opportunities to learn patience. We aren't given kindness toward others; we are given opportunities to share kindness when someone doesn't deserve it. We aren't just given joy or gentleness; we are given the opportunity to grow amid chaos and respond according to God's ways. Refinement doesn't happen unless we're willing to draw our line in the sand, burn our ships, and fully follow God. We can't be double-minded. We're either all in or we're all out.

> *We're either all in or we're all out.*

Each of us daily faces opportunities where we can choose to get ahead by the world's ways, but we aren't called to walk according to the world—we're called to a higher standard. I've had plenty of opportunities to get ahead in ways that were contradictory to God's ways, whether that's the time someone tried to pay me a reduced contract amount in cash to avoid taxes (I declined, our company always does business honorably) or by cutting corners in the building process to save time or money (we haven't and we won't). I've experienced my share of personal and professional struggles. Still, I remain convinced that the successes I've seen are due to choosing the path of integrity in my decision to work in God's economy regardless of what the world says.

> *We aren't called to walk according to the world—we're called to a higher standard.*

So here's the question—are you willing to burn your ships? Stop and consult with God, who knows you the best and loves you the most. Instead of asking God to get behind your plans, ask Him first what He wants you to pursue. Ask Him what ships you need to burn to focus on His plan entirely. Is it a destructive habit or an unhealthy relationship? Is it personal ambition? A tendency to save money for yourself and resist faithful giving? Addictions? Questionable business dealings? The list can be endless.

> *Instead of asking God to get behind your plans, ask Him first what He wants you to pursue.*

Burning your ships will require something of you. Whether you seek a new path or need to step away from an addiction, bad habit, or event, you need to be fully committed to walking away from the past with no thoughts of returning to it or thinking you can dabble back and forth. It won't exempt you from times of uncertainty or waiting. We are all in some season of waiting or transition. But can we serve others faithfully even when we feel out of place? Will we turn into the storms we face and walk boldly through them to fulfill God's calling on our lives? Do we have the wisdom to choose what's important over what's pressing? Do we have the boldness to obey God even when His promise(s) seem outlandish or so far from completion? Will we be persistent in pursuing God's ways despite what the world thinks? Will we allow circumstance to overwhelm us, or will we remember all that God has previously done in, through, and for us and allow it to sustain us in our waiting?

Burning your ships isn't easy, but it will empower you to wait confidently, knowing that regardless of what season you are in or what door God has brought you to you are fully equipped to step forward with both feet firmly in God's ways.

Remember, God's plans are exceedingly and abundantly more than we can imagine (Eph. 3:20). Burning your ships isn't easy, but it will empower you to wait confidently. You will have confidence knowing that regardless of what season you are in or what door God has brought you to, you are fully equipped to step forward with both feet firmly in God's ways, eyes focused on Him, and fully equipped for all that's ahead. It's a walk of faith that's well worth the journey if you're willing to take it.

Takeaways

1. Stay focused on the road ahead of you and avoid looking back and being double-minded at all costs.

2. Refinement doesn't happen without a refining fire, through which we are granted opportunities to learn what we desire the most.

3. Instead of asking God to bless your current plans, first ask Him what He wants you to pursue.

Reflections

1. Are you currently or have you ever tried living with one eye on God and another on the world? What was the result?

_____

_____

_____

_____

_____

2. What ships (events, addictions, habits, or relationships) do you need to burn to fully step into what God has for you? Please take a moment to list them out. If you're struggling to think of anything, ask someone you trust for their honest insight.

_____

_____

_____

_____

_____

_____

3. Have you ever considered that the Fruit of the Spirit is grown by you, not just given? How can you choose to ensure that you're tending to your garden daily?

_____

_____

_____

_____

_____

_____

12

Crossing the
Final Threshold

We all will leave this earth one day, but we don't know when or how. Some will leave suddenly because of a tragic accident or illness. But some will face a period of waiting.

Within six months, my wife Carol's mom and both of my parents were promoted to heaven. During their last years, months, days, and hours, we were an intimate part of their final wait and crossing the threshold into heaven. We spent many years caring for our parents when they could no longer care for themselves. I can't imagine how difficult it was for them, and it was frustrating for Carol and me because we couldn't fix anything.

Whether we like it or not, our own time will come, and each of us will come face to face with our mortality and the fact that our days are indeed numbered. This is why the liminal space, the place of transition and in-between, is so important. It can bring us face-to-face with who we are, how we show up in the world, our strengths and vulnerabilities, and our successes and disappointments. It can cause us to reflect on our beliefs, practices, and identity of who we are or have become and how we have treated others, including our family, throughout life.

This is why the liminal space, the place of transition and in between, is so important. It can bring us face-to-face with who we are, how we show up in the world, our strengths and vulnerabilities, our successes and disappointments.

I can't stress enough the importance of being still, looking, listening, and understanding what is happening around you and in you. These waiting times and transitions along our journey prepare us for how we will approach what lies beyond the threshold of whatever door of opportunity God provides. But they also point toward our lives being spent in a more significant liminal space, preparing us for what's on the other side of this life.

What did we do in the numbered days given to us? Will we be faithful to the end? Will we represent God in all our words, attitudes, and responses in the face of the unknown? Will we reflect God's faithfulness and a heart of gratitude for all that He's allowed us to experience in life? It seems to me that it'd be better to meet this transition, having lived a life of fullness rather than with regrets over what we should have done.

It can be easy to neglect time alone or to slow down to be still or quiet, but we must all step out of the daily grind of life to take stock of what's necessary and what can be set aside. We need to ask the tough questions. Considering

Crossing the Final Threshold

where God wants me to be, what should I focus on to get there? Am I incorporating the right things to help me finish strong? Will I be alone or surrounded by those who love and support me? How can I build those relationships daily?

Unfortunately, taking this time to slow down won't just happen on its own—we must intentionally plan it into our schedule, or something else will always seek to take its place.

I lived in a converted 8'x8' storage room at my parent's home in my early years of starting a business. It makes me think about how we often plan to upgrade from living in one room containing all our earthly possessions to purchasing a larger home to accommodate a growing family. We downsize when children grow up and leave to make things more manageable. If we live long enough, we may end up in one room that holds us and all our earthly possessions again.

Does what we collect along the way matter? Is it still with us? Often, it's our Bible, favorite book(s), photos, memories, and letters. But when we leave this earth, none of it will go with us. Our children, friends, or even strangers may rifle through our home, determining what goes to family or goodwill or is put in the garbage can. What's left has meaning because of the memories and life associated with it—when we are gone. Those memories can quickly fade if family and friends don't share along the way.

Carol and I and others cared for our aging parents, and we cherished recounting past experiences. Though my mom struggled with dementia and Carol's mom with Alzheimer's, we still connected with them on our shared history. Sometimes we have to go back many years to connect with what's going on in their minds. Each day was constantly changing because of the unpredictable reality of the disease. Photo albums sometimes helped them recall and remember people or events.

We chose to see life through their eyes since they could no longer keep up with the present. We told stories of family events and watched them closely to see if they recalled them. If not, we would move on to another memory so that it was not awkward for them or they did not have to struggle mentally to grasp something that was no longer there. As we spoke, sometimes their eyes would light up with remembrance, and it was a joyous occasion.

> ## Honor the relationships in your life now, while you still have time.

I share our experience with our parents as a reminder to honor the relationships in your life now while you still have time. We never know when someone's light will be extinguished and we'll have missed our moment to apologize, forgive, and love well. If you've missed a moment with someone in your life, learn to forgive yourself and make sure you're prepared for the next moment. I wish Carol and I had begun sooner, but we pressed into the time we had left with our parents, taking the time to record videos of them sharing stories for future generations in our family. We read Scripture and books to them, sharing moments of comfort, peace, laughter, and love.

Our parents stayed true to who they were and what they believed. During most of our time together toward the end, we would pray for them, and I was amazed that they would spend their time praying for me and whoever else was in the room. We did our best to keep their favorite artist's music playing, and the song in their heart of laughter, love, encouragement, and spirit stayed joyful and hopeful until the end.

Though one day we will all be gone, God's Word and His love last forever—steep yourself in them:

> The grass withers and the flowers fade,
>   but the word of our God stands forever.
> (Isa. 40:8 NLT)

> Give thanks to the LORD, for he is good.
>   His love endures forever.
> Give thanks to the God of gods.
>   His love endures forever.
> Give thanks to the Lord of lords:
>   His love endures forever.
> To him who alone does great wonders,
>   His love endures forever. (Ps. 136:1-4 NIV)

Carol's aunt didn't know what lay ahead when she stepped onto an airplane headed toward a new life in Australia as a young woman. But she was confident she would arrive at her destination with her husband and that God's plan would unfold accordingly. Later in life, as she was preparing to make the trip home to Heaven, she was confident in knowing her destination and that God is still faithful.

As my dad approached death, I witnessed a special moment when he looked up and held up his arm as if he was letting God know he was ready. There wasn't an ounce of fear in him. He was tired and knew his body had given out, but Dad was prepared to take on his heavenly body with no more sorrow or tears.

He was ready to forever be with God, with the One who died in his place so he could have eternal life. Nothing left on earth could compare or compel him to want to stay any longer.

I think about the close relationship I developed over a lifetime with my father and am reminded that it's an example of what God wants for us. He wants us to do life together, to share the journey with others. The wins and losses, the detours, and the waiting are all part of our story, and what we face and how we respond prepares us to walk confidently toward our future.

We realize that everyone who will reach our final threshold of waiting will have a definitive transition from this world to the next. We were blessed to hold our parents' hands as they passed to Heaven, and I couldn't help but wonder who else's hand I might hold as they did the same. Who will be holding mine? As we are left behind, it's still natural to mourn the loss of our loved ones. But we grieve with hope and joy for the life we've shared and with determination to finish our race well. The day we were born, God also knew the story of our lives, the waiting seasons that would come, and the final culmination of our days when we would breathe our last breath. He knew the purpose and plan that we would live our lives to bring honor and glory to Him.

Though it can seem overwhelming, each of our lives matters and has an eternal impact—we are an example to those around us. How we wait in life, press into God, and how hope for the future can and will make a difference in the lives of others. How we face eternity matters. Do we face it with joy, knowing we are close to seeing God face to face? Do we give final encouraging words to those we are leaving behind? Are we afraid, or do we live with the hope of Heaven in response to the reality that each of us will one day face this time of liminality?

My prayer for us all is that God would "teach us to number our days, that we may gain a heart of wisdom" (Ps. 90:12 NIV). We will cross the final threshold, whether we are prepared or not. What we do with this life determines where we will step into, and in one moment, the consequences of our choices will live for eternity. Choose now and choose wisely—none of us knows when we may draw our last breath.

Alan Redpath, a well-known British evangelist, pastor, and author, said, "The conversion of a soul is the miracle of the moment, but the manufacture of a saint is the task of a lifetime." If you are waiting to hear about a job application, a raise, your paycheck, the baby to stop crying, trying to determine your next season, or waiting for life to begin or end, you are not alone. A cloud of witnesses surrounds you—don't quit! No matter where you are in your race or what you are waiting on, know that you are not alone and will make it.

Takeaways

1. Stay true to who God created you to be. He wants you to be the best version of yourself.

2. Be a positive, engaged, and enthusiastic example. Your life matters, and you can make an eternal impact.

3. Honor the relationships you have in your life while you can encourage, impart, and embark on projects or adventures together.

4. Our days are numbered—make the most of each one.

Reflections

1. Have you considered how our lives are spent in one liminal space or another in preparation for what comes after this life? What does this mean to you?

_____

_____

_____

_____

_____

2. Have you considered how you wait and respond in your life could permanently impact someone else as you grow in your faith? Does this change your perspective as a Christian on how you view and respond to every person you meet or business opportunity that crosses your path daily?

_____

_____

_____

_____

_____

_____

3. Whose hand are you holding? How are you cheering on and encouraging those around you? Ultimately, who will be holding your hand as you wait to pass into the hands of the Father?

_____

_____

_____

_____

_____

Conclusion

Have you ever imagined how God must feel when it comes to waiting?

He created a magnificent world, and His final decision was to create man to enjoy the world with Him and care for it. How soon was it, though, until Eve and Adam did the only thing He told them not to do? They messed that gift up by not understanding what they had and how they were to experience it.

God was so upset with how man continued to interpret creation and how to utilize and enjoy it that He destroyed everyone but Noah and his family. He made a way for Noah's family to be saved because they were faithful to Him.

Yet God still loved those He had created in His image. He wanted to enjoy life with us. He gave direction and provision to live life and fully experience it in His ways and according to His purposes. And yet we all continued to mess it up and misinterpret His intentions.

He finally sent His only Son to show us the way. He paid the price with His life for us—past, present, and future. And yet, He is still waiting for us to understand what He has done for us and how He wanted to enjoy His creation with us.

References

While writing this book, several resources inspired and informed my writing. Of note are the Olive Tree Bible app and the numerous resources available through the software:

- For Everyone Commentary Series
- *The MacArthur Bible Handbook*
- The Message Bible
- *Preach the Word* (Stephen Oliver Stout)
- Preacher Commentary Series

I also found great encouragement and fresh insights through Matthew Henry's *Concise Commentary on the Whole Bible*, *The Maxwell Leadership Bible (3rd Edition)*, Charles Swindoll's "Insights on Matthew" and "Insights on Luke" found in Swindoll's *Living Insights New Testament Commentary* Books 1 and 3, and *The Blackaby Study Bible* (NKJV).

Additional Resources Cited Throughout

AA San Juan. "The Challenges of Failure." *Daily Reflections*. Alcoholics Anonymous San Juan. Accessed July 2, 2022. AA Daily Reflections — Condado 12 & 12 | Alcoholics Anonymous in San Juan, Puerto Rico. https://www.aasanjuan.org/.

Bruce, F.F. "God's Amazing Work, Ephesians 2:10." *Preaching the Word Commentary*. Holy Bible App, Gospel Technologies LLC, Vers. 7.10.8, 2021. Apple App Store. apps.apple.com/us/app/Bible-app-read-study-daily/id332615624.

Chambers, Oswald. "If You Will Ask: Reflections on the Power of Prayer (Signature Collection)." Our Daily Bread. Our Daily Bread Publishing. Kindle Edition, p. 27.

Detrick, Hallie. "A Picasso Painting Owned by Steve Wynn Was Damaged — Again." *Fortune*. 14 May 2018. http://fortune.com/2018/05/14/steve-wynn-picasso-painting/.

Evans, Tony. "Saved to Serve, Ephesians 2:1-10." *Tony Evans Bible Commentary, Section IV. Holy Bible App.* Gospel Technologies LLC, Vers. 7.10.8, 2021. *Apple App Store. apps.apple.com/us/app/Bible-app-read-study-daily/id332615624.*

Hodge, Bodie. "How Long Did It Take for Noah to Build the Ark?" *Answers in Genesis*. 23 May 2018. https://answersingenesis.org/Bible-timeline/how-long-did-it-take-for-noah-to-build-the-ark/.

References

O'Toole, Garson. "Dear Quote Investigator: Dwight E. Eisenhower." *Quote Investigator.* 9 May 2014. https://quoteinvestigator.com/2014/05/09/urgent/.

Redpath, Alan. *The Making of a Man of God: Lessons from the Life of David.* Michigan: Baker Publishing Group, Revell, 2004.

Simmons III, Richard E. *The True Measure of a Man, How Perceptions of Success, Achievement & Recognition Fail Men in Difficult Times.* Kindle. Alabama: Evergreen Press, 2013.

Surowiecki, James. "Hanging Tough." *The New Yorker.* 13 April 2009. www.newyorker.com/magazine/2009/04/20/hanging-tough.

Zimmer, John. "Burning the Ships and Sailing Away." *Manner of Speaking.* 3 January 2015. https://mannerofspeaking.org/2015/01/03/burning-the-ships-and-sailing-away/.

Suggested Reading

Leadership on the Level

Many problems plague even the most successful leaders. In leadership, you will always carry a weight, and it must be balanced. In *Leadership on the Level*, Jerry shares the keys to achieving balanced leadership.

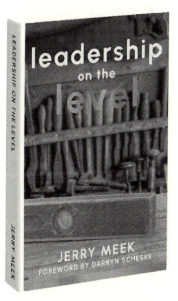

Through a guided tour of the well-known "Sermon on the Mount," you'll uncover how your internal motivations play out in your life and the organizations you lead. By taking an architectural review of the blueprints in the gospel and applying it to your life, you'll come away with:

- A real-world application of scripture and teaching for your everyday life

- A roadmap for aligning your life and organization to purpose, plan, and orchestrated execution

- How to bring the right people on the team and create a thriving culture

- How to stay true to your vision and values (i.e., maintain your integrity), especially through seasons of change and hardship

It's time to start leading on the level that you were created to—causing yourself and those around you to thrive and live the abundant life available to everyone.

Be Great... Before It's Too Late

It doesn't matter whether you are eight or eighty-eight—ordinary can become extraordinary with just a little extra effort, thought, planning, and perspective. In life, we have many opportunities to win or to lose. We are faced with a constant choice: we can become more or remain the same.

Are you living a life on its way to being great or a life that will fall short of your ultimate destiny?

In *Be Great...Before It's Too Late*, Jerry dives deep into the stories of some of the most inspiring men and women in history and explores their valleys and peaks. You will see the benefits of their discipline and the rewards of finishing the race, and you will be reminded of the importance of beginning with purpose and finishing strong.

This book is an invitation to a journey to discover what a life of greatness could look like. While you still have time and a future to experience, what can make the difference in your own life so that you can discover and experience a life of greatness?

Team Builder Toolbox

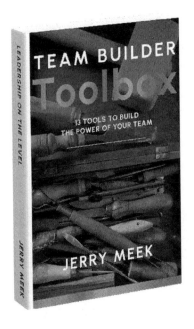

Your team's most significant successes are built with powerful tools. These essential tools can be collected and shared like a builder's toolbox. Each tool has its unique purpose, from sharpening leadership skills and refining character to stimulating creativity and advancing personal and professional integrity.

In *Team Builder Toolbox*, Jerry outlines thirteen tools your business needs. These tools were carefully crafted and implemented over time with the same enduring standard of excellence that has been used to build some of the world's most distinguished residential and commercial projects. From the moment you discover these tools for yourself, your best results will connect with your hopes and dreams as they lay the foundation of what you and your team build together today and for the future.

Join the Glorious Reflections Community

Glorious Reflections helps overwhelmed marketplace leaders rediscover their eternal purpose and earthly mission. Led by Jerry Meek, the community is a collective of leaders who desire to live and lead in a way that reflects the glory of God. Jerry is a leader who has been in your shoes and has seen firsthand the power of living a life totally surrendered to God. He is now devoted to helping others do the same.

When we understand that the most authentic person we can be and the most impactful work we can do is found in the One we reflect, we are empowered to live a life of perspective and purpose.

You are invited to join us on the journey so you, too, can live and lead in a way that reflects all of who He is and who you've been created to be.

while YOU wait

Sign Up to Join the Community

Take the Challenge:
21 Days to Living and Leading in a Way That Reflects the Glory of God

Some people are talented—they're great at doing something, but they're not great at being someone. As a leader, are you making decisions out of your own strength on an empty tank? Or are you seeking God first in prayer, gaining His perspective and making decisions that best align with His purpose for your life? This 21-Day Reflections Challenge is designed to help you do just that.

Our gift to you — register for this email series and you will receive a downloadable PDF to print and fill out each day of the challenge, along with a daily email to guide you through the reflection process. At the end of 21 days, you will feel more empowered and focused as a leader.

By taking the challenge, you will:

- Uncover the role your faith plays in your leadership

- Establish a healthy habit of reflection to start your day

- Gain perspective on the deep meaning and purpose of what your life can truly become

Sign Up to Take the Challenge

About the Author

Jerry Meek is the Founder & CEO of Desert Star Construction, known by clients and industry colleagues as "the best team in the luxury home business," and Glorious Reflections, an online community that helps overwhelmed Christian marketplace leaders rediscover their eternal purpose and find unending joy in their life and leadership.

Jerry's last decade has been focused on the continuous growth and expansion of Team DSC®. The results have been published in more than thirty magazines and earned honors such as multiple Gold Nugget Awards, Phoenix Home & Garden Home of the Year, Southwest Contractor, and NAHB Custom Home of the Year. In 2017, Jerry was the first-ever luxury custom home builder to receive Phoenix Home & Garden's Master of the Southwest, an award program in its thirtieth year that recognizes the best in design and craftsmanship. Jerry also served as the founding president of the Phoenix Dream Center Foundation, which aids young survivors of human trafficking.

Today, Jerry continues to enjoy life's journey with Carol, his wife of over forty years, in Cave Creek, Arizona, and his adult children, Jeremy (wife, Yasaman) and Jonathan.

You can join Jerry's online community, Glorious Reflections, and follow Jerry on social media by visiting these links:

jerryrmeek.com | /jerryrmeek
@jerryrmeek | /jerryrmeek